FILUMENA MARTURANO
A Mother's a Mother

I0139741

Eduardo de Filippo
English Version by
Eric Bentley

BROADWAY PLAY PUBLISHING INC
New York
www.broadwayplaypublishing.com
info@broadwayplaypublishing.com

FILUMENA MARTURANO
© Copyright 1953 by Eric Bentley and the Franz J
Horch Agency

Cover art by Lamont O'Neal

First edition: July 2017
I S B N: 978-0-88145-709-4

Book design: Marie Donovan
Page make-up: Adobe InDesign
Typeface: Palatino

CHARACTERS & SETTING

FILUMENA MARTURANO
DOMENICO SORIANO
ALFREDO AMOROSO, DOMENICO's *crony*
ROSALIA, FILUMENA's *friend*
DIANA, DOMENICO's *mistress*
LUCIA, *the maid*
UMBERTO, FILUMENA's *son*
RICCARDO, FILUMENA's *son*
MICHELE, FILUMENA's *son*
NOCELLA, *a lawyer*
TERESINA, *a seamstress*
two WAITERS

The Place: Naples
The Time: Not long ago

ACT ONE

(*The style of* Domenico'*s dining room is decidedly
twentieth century. The room is showily furnished in
mediocre taste. Certain pictures and ornaments, carefully
placed on the walls and furnishings, violently conflict with
this modernism. They doubtless belonged to his father.*)

(*The door downstage left leads to the bedroom. Upstairs left,
a large French window set across the corner of the room
looks out on an ample terrace that is provided with plants
and flowers and shaded by a colored, striped awning. The
main door is in the back wall on the right. Upstage right
there is an archway; and through partly drawn curtains
one can descry what* Domenico *dares to call his study.
Here also his penchant for modernity shows itself. It is a
"modern" cabinet which protects and exhibits a vast number
of cups of various metals and divers forms and dimensions;
these are the First Prizes his racehorses have won.*)

(*On the opposite wall, behind a desk, two crossed banners
bear witness to victories at the Festa di Montevergine. Not
a book, not a journal, not even a piece of paper. The study is
orderly and decent, but lifeless.*)

(*In the center of the dining room is a table laid with
considerable care and taste for two. In the middle are fresh
red roses.*)

(*It is the time of year when spring is turning into summer.
It is the time of day when afternoon is turning into evening.
The sun is shedding its last rays on the terrace.*)

*(At rise: Four people are on stage—*FILUMENA, DOMENICO, ROSALIA, *and* ALFREDO.*)*

*(*FILUMENA *is wearing a long white nightgown. Her hair is in disorder, though a hasty attempt has been made to set it to rights. Her feet are stockingless in her old bedroom slippers. This woman's face shows signs of torment: we can see her past has been sad and stormy. Filumena doesn't look coarse, but she cannot hide her humble origin, nor would she want to. Her gestures are broad and open. Her tone of voice is candid and forceful: she is someone to reckon with, rich in instinctive intelligence and moral force. After her own fashion she knows life and its laws—and after her own fashion confronts them. A strand or two of silver on the temples announce her forty-eight years; not so her dark eyes, which have preserved all the youthful vitality of the dark Neapolitan type. She is pale as a corpse, partly from the role she has just been playing [she has pretended to be dying], partly because of the storm she knows is coming. But she isn't afraid. On the contrary, she is waiting like some wounded beast to leap on her adversary.)*

*(*DOMENICO *is a strong, healthy man of about fifty. He has lived well. Money and an easy time of it have kept him lively in spirit and youthful in appearance. His father, Raimondo Soriano, was one of the richest and most rascally confectioners in Naples; he had bakeries at Vergini and Forcella and very popular stores in Toledo and Foria. And* DOMENICO *was the apple of his eye. The caprices of* DON DOMENICO—*as a boy he was Signorino Don Mimi—knew no bounds either for originality or extravagance; they were famous and even today are the talk of Naples. A passionate horse fancier, he can spend half the day with his cronies going over the athletic feats of the leading champions who have passed through his well-fed stables. And now here he is, wearing only a pair of pants and a quickly buttoned house jacket, pale, convulsed, facing this "thing of naught,"* FILUMENA *, whom for so many years he has treated as a*

slave, but who now holds him in the palm of her hand, ready
to crush him like an insect. Not that he knows it; he sees no
limits to his will. He is sure of the triumph of his godlike
reason. He is sure he can expose the outrage, lay bare before
the world the baseness which has deceived him. He feels
offended, insulted, and, in a certain sense which he can't
explain and wouldn't if he could, desecrated. The fact that
he seems publicly discomfited turns his head; he is going
berserk.)

(ROSALIA is mild and humble. She is seventy-five. Her hair
is of an uncertain color, rather more white than gray. She
is wearing a dark dress of no definite color. A little bent
but still full of life. She used to live in a basso—the name
the Neapolitans give to ground floor living quarters in the
slums. This was in San Liborio Street, right opposite where
the MARTURANOS lived: that's how she came to know
all about them. She has known FILUMENA from earliest
childhood. She was with her in her saddest moments, and
did not spare those words of comfort, understanding, and
tenderness which the common women of Italy have to offer,
and which are a balsam to the suffering heart. From harsh
experience she knows the effects of this man's irascibility and
is petrified.)

(ALFREDO is an agreeable fellow of some seventy years,
solidly built, vigorous, muscular. He was a fine coachman,
and it was in this capacity that DOMENICO first took him on,
keeping him ever after at his side as handyman, scapegoat,
spy, and friend. He has come to symbolize his master's past.
You can see how loyal and devoted he is to DOMENICO, and
how great his self-abnegation, in the way his eyes follow his
master. He is wearing a gray jacket of perfect cut, if a little
frayed, trousers of another color, and a beret worn jauntily
on one side. On his portly belly he displays a gold chain. He
is simply waiting—perhaps the calmest of the four people in
the room, for he knows his DOMENICO, he hasn't fetched and
carried for him for nothing.)

(As the scene opens, FILUMENA *is standing by the bedroom door with her arms folded, a posture of defiance. Downstage right is* DOMENICO, *facing her. Upstage left, near the terrace, stands* ROSALIA. *Upstage right is* ALFREDO. *They are standing in the four corners of the room as if playing a children's game. A long pause)*

DOMENICO: *(Slapping himself repeatedly, vehemently)* Fool! Fool! Fool!!!

ALFREDO: *(Intervening with a slight gesture)* Now really, Don Do…

DOMENICO: Am I a man? I should go to a mirror and spit in my face! *(To* FILUMENA*)* Married to you? I've wasted a lifetime with you already: twenty-five years of health and strength and youth and effort! And you want that, too? And Don Domenico has no choice but to give it to you? For twenty-five years you've done what you liked with me, you've all done what you liked with me! *(To himself)* You thought you were Jesus Christ our Lord, and they've all done what they liked with you! *(He turns to the three of them one after the other.)* You, you, you—in our street—in our precinct—in Naples—throughout the world—you've planned my downfall! *(Now he is quiet again.)* It won't bear thinking about. But I might have known. A woman like you *had* to get where you've got. But don't think you've heard the last of this. I'll murder you! And all your accomplices, too! The doctor, the priest, and *(Pointing at* ROSALIA *and* ALFREDO*)* those two reprobates who've lived off me and grown fat off me, I'll murder you all! *(Looks for his revolver)* Where's my revolver? Give me my revolver.

ALFREDO: *(Calmly)* It's at the gun shop. I took it to be cleaned. Like you told me.

DOMENICO: I've told you plenty in my time, haven't I? And it's beginning to look as if I was telling you what

you wanted me to tell you, isn't it? Well, that's all over:
My eyes have been opened! *(To* FILUMENA*)* You will
leave this house. And if you don't leave quietly, you'll
leave dead. No law can stop me! No *God* can stop
Domenico Soriano!! I'll denounce you in the streets,
I'll send you to the galleys! I can pay the piper and I'll
call the tune! And when I tell them who you were and
where you lived when I picked you up, I'll win my
case all right! I'll annihilate you!!

(Pause)

FILUMENA: *(Not at all overwhelmed, sure of herself)* Are
you through now?

DOMENICO: *(Still roaring)* And don't speak to me. I can't
stand it!!!

FILUMENA: *(Calmly)* When I've said my say, I'll never
set eyes on you again. And you'll never hear my voice
again.

DOMENICO: *(Still bellowing)* A harlot: that's what you
were and that's what you are!!!!

FILUMENA: *(Still quiet)* Why do you shout so? It's no
secret. Everyone knows who I was and where I lived.
But—you—came—there. Like the others. And I treated
you like the others. Why should I treat you different:
aren't men created equal? What I've done…well, I'm
sorry for it. But now I'm your wife, Domenico. The
army and the navy can't change that.

DOMENICO: My—wife?

FILUMENA: Your wife.

DOMENICO: You're crazy! It was the most barefaced
piece of trickery you ever heard of. You were sick,
were you? You must take to your deathbed, must you?
A trick: and I have witnesses! *(He indicates* ROSALIA *and*
ALFREDO.*)*

ROSALIA: *(Hastily, not wanting to be dragged in)* I know nothing. All I know is, Donna Filumena got sick, she got so bad she was going to die, but she never said nothing. I know nothing neither.

DOMENICO: *(To* ALFREDO*)* You know nothing either, huh? You didn't know this dying was just an act?

ALFREDO: By the Holy Virgin, Don Mimi! If Donna Filumena wanted to tell somebody, it certainly wouldn't be me: she can't stand the sight of me!

ROSALIA: What about the priest? Who told me to call the priest? You did!

DOMENICO: Because she wanted him…I wanted to please her…

FILUMENA: Oh, of course—you didn't believe I was passing on, did you? Oh, no! You weren't thinking how nice it would be to get rid of me, were you?

DOMENICO: Yes, I was! And you were whispering in the priest's ear. And the priest said, "Marry her! Marry her in extremis, poor woman! It is her one remaining wish! With the good Lord's blessing, tie the bridal knot!!"

FILUMENA: And you said to yourself, "After all, what have I got to lose? It's only a question of hours, it won't cost much." When the priest left, I hopped out of bed and said, "Wish us luck, Domenico, for now—we're husband and wife!" It must have been quite a shock.

ROSALIA: *(Hysterical)* I nearly jumped out of my skin. And laugh! I couldn't stop! *(In fact, she starts again.)* I can't get over it, I could have sworn she was sick…

ALFREDO: On her deathbed in fact…

DOMENICO: If you two don't be quiet, *you'll* be on your deathbed!! *(Pausing)* But I still don't get it: how could she… *(He has a thought.)* What about the doctor? A qualified doctor could come here and not notice she's in perfect health and making a fool of him?

ALFREDO: I think…er…maybe he made a mistake.

DOMENICO: *(Stung)* Shut up. Alfredo! *(Thinking hard)* That doctor needn't think he'll get away with it, he'll pay for this as sure as God's in heaven! He couldn't have acted in good faith, he was in on the deal sure as fate, *you* cut him in on it, you *bought* him, huh?

FILUMENA: Bought! The only idea in your head: everything you ever wanted you bought. Including me. Because you were Don—Mimi—Soriano. You wore the best shirts, you went to the best tailors, your race horses ran for you, and you did quite a bit of running yourself, didn't you, after one thing and another? And sometimes I set the pace, Don Mimi, and you didn't know it, and you've a long way to run yet, Don Mimi, there's blood and sweat ahead, before—you— know—what—a—gentleman—is! *(She is quiet again now.)* The doctor knew nothing about it, he thought I was dying, too: why shouldn't he? *(Another change of tone)* Any woman would be on her deathbed after twenty-five years with you. *(To* ROSALIA *and* ALFREDO*)* For twenty-five years I've been his servant. You know that. He just used to go away and have a good time. In London. In Paris. Or at the race tracks. So I was his policeman. I went to the bakeries at Forcella and Vergini, I went to the stores in Toledo and Foria. If I hadn't he'd have been robbed right and left. *(She imitates his hypocritical tone.)* "I don't know what I'd do without you, Filumena, you're—a woman!" *(Shouting)* I've kept house for him better than a…a legitimate wife! *(Dropping her voice)* I've washed his feet. Not just since I've got old. Even when I was young—I washed his feet. *(Raising her voice again)* I might have been a housemaid he could fire from one moment to the next!

DOMENICO: *(Sullenly)* You never tried to understand how things stood between us. Always mooning around the house with that sullen, resentful face. You said to yourself, "Well am I in the wrong? Have I done anything to him?" *(Slowly)* I have never seen a tear in those eyes. Never. In all the years we've lived through together, I have never seen her cry!

FILUMENA: I should have cried then? For you maybe? For this fine…

DOMENICO: Never mind about me. You were a soul in torment that knew no peace! A woman who doesn't cry, doesn't eat, doesn't sleep—I never saw you sleep but once! A damned soul, that's you!

FILUMENA: When did you want to see me sleep? You never came home. I was always alone. Even at Easter. Even at Christmas. Like a lonely old dog. Do you know when a woman cries. Don Mimi? When she catches sight of the good thing and can't have it. Filumena never caught sight of the good thing. And when all you know is the bad thing, you don't cry. It's good to cry, I know that, crying is a blessing, a blessing Filumena wasn't to know. A harlot you call me, and well you might—you always treated me as one. *(To* ROSALIA *and* ALFREDO, *sole witnesses of the sacred truth of what she is saying.)* And let's not talk of his youth and his wild oats. In those days you could say, "Well, he's rich, he's spoiled, he'll get over it". But now he's fifty-two and he still comes home with lipstick on his handkerchiefs. Pah! Where are they, Rosalia?

ROSALIA: *(Reassuringly)* In the cupboard, Donna Filumena.

FILUMENA: A considerate man would say to himself, "She mustn't find them, I must hide them someplace". What this man thought was, "What can she do when

she finds them? Who is she, anyway? What rights has
she?" And off he goes after his little…

DOMENICO: *(Caught out and furious)* His little—who?

FILUMENA: *(Not in the least intimidated, more violent than
he)* …after his little floozy! You think I didn't catch
on? You can't even tell good lies, that's what's wrong
with you. Fifty-two years old and he's still after girls
of *twenty*-two! He isn't ashamed of himself either. He
sets her up in *my* home. We all pretend she's a nurse.
Because he believed—oh, yes, he believed—I was
dying. *(This is true but incredible.)* Not more than one
hour ago, before the priest came to marry us, they
thought I was just going to give my soul to God, and
I'd lost my sense of sight, so, at the foot of *my* bed,
they started kissing and caressing!… (*She can't hold her
nausea back.)* Madonna, you make me fee! sick to the
stomach! Why, suppose I'd *really* been dying—with
you carrying on like that at the foot of my bed!! Me
dying in there, the table laid in here. For two: him and
the corpse, I suppose!

DOMENICO: You mean, when you're dying, I'm not
supposed to eat? I had to have food, didn't I?

FILUMENA: With roses on the table?

DOMENICO: *(Passing it off as normal)* With roses on the
table.

FILUMENA: Red roses?

DOMENICO: *(Losing patience)* Red, blue, green, good
God, can't I have roses if I want to? *(He is blustering
now.)* If I want to, can't I be glad you're dead?

FILUMENA: Only I'm not dead, Domenico. *(Defiantly)* I
changed my mind.

DOMENICO: *(To himself)* "So put that in your pipe and
smoke it." *(Pause)* But there's something I don't get. If
you've always treated me just like all the others, if men

are all alike, if, as you put it, they're created equal, why did you have to marry me? And if I'm in love with this girl and want to marry her—and I will marry Diana, mark my words—what does it matter to you whether she's twenty or a hundred and fifty?

FILUMENA: You're right: that girl doesn't matter. *(She buckles down to explain.)* Did you really think I'd done it for you? You didn't enter into my calculations at all. You never have. A woman of my type—you've said it yourself, you've always said it—a woman like me has it all figured. *(Underlining each word)* It so happens I can use you. *(A break)* Or did you really believe—after the lifetime of sacrifice I've lived—that I'd simply pick up and go?

DOMENICO: *(Thinking he understands, jubilant)* Money! I knew it! But couldn't you have had it? *(Pompously)* You think a son of the Sorianos would have failed to provide for you? Failed to set you up in a home of your own? Failed to make you a woman of independent means?

FILUMENA: *(Humiliated by his lack of understanding, with scorn)* Oh, stop! Will you men never understand anything? As for your money, Domenico, you can keep it. Keep it. It's something else I want of you right now. And you're going to give it to me. *(Pause)* I have three sons.

(DOMENICO and ALFREDO are astonished. ROSALIA is not.)

DOMENICO: Three sons? What are you talking about, Filumena?

FILUMENA: *(Repeating herself almost mechanically)* I have three sons.

DOMENICO: *(Bewildered)* But…whose children are they?

FILUMENA: *(What DOMENICO fears, not having escaped her, coldly)* Their fathers are men like you.

DOMENICO: (*Gravely*) Filumena, Filumena, you're playing with fire. What do you mean, men like me?

FILUMENA: Men are created equal.

DOMENICO: (*To* ROSALIA) You *knew* about this?

ROSALIA: (*Feelingly*) I certainly did!

DOMENICO: (*To* ALFREDO) You, too?

ALFREDO: (*Eager to get out of it*) No! Donna Filumena hates me. I told you!

DOMENICO: (*Not yet convinced, as if to himself*) Three sons?

FILUMENA: The eldest is twenty-six.

DOMENICO: Twenty-six?

FILUMENA: You needn't pull such a face about it. They're not yours.

DOMENICO: (*Somewhat relieved*) Do they know you? Do they see you? Do they know you're their mother?

FILUMENA: No, but *I* see *them*. Often. I talk to them.

DOMENICO: What do they do? Where do they live? What do they live *on*?

FILUMENA: They live on your money.

DOMENICO: (*Surprised*) They live on my money?

FILUMENA: They live on your money. I stole it from you. From your wallet when necessary. Under your very nose.

DOMENICO: So you're a thief!

FILUMENA: (*Boldly*) I sold your suits, I sold your shoes, you never noticed. Remember that diamond ring? I said it was lost? Well, I'd sold it. I've raised my family on your money. I'm a thief.

DOMENICO: (*Appalled*) What sort of woman *are* you?

FILUMENA: *(Goes on as if he hadn't spoken)* One of them has a store in the next street. He's a plumber.

ROSALIA: *(Correcting her)* An engineer: sanitary and high-droolic!

DOMENICO: *(Who hasn't followed this)* What!?

ROSALIA: *(Pronouncing the word right this time)* A sanitary and *hydraulic* engineer! Fixes faucets and all that… The second boy, what's his name? *(Searches for the name)* Riccardo…he's the handsome one, a real lady killer, lives on Via Chiaia, he has a shop too, number seventy-four, he's a shirtmaker, and what shirts, and what customers… Then, there's Umberto.

FILUMENA: He wants to study. He's always wanted to study. He's a thinker! Writes in the papers!

DOMENICO: *(Ironically)* So we have a writer in the family.

ROSALIA: And what a mother she's made them! They've never wanted for anything. I am old and I may find myself at any moment in the presence of Him who beholdeth all things, comprehendeth all things, and forgiveth all things, so it's true, what I say, and don't you go listening to no gossip! From the time they was in their baby clothes, she's fed them on milk and honey!

DOMENICO: Paid for with Don Domenico's shirts, shoes, and diamond rings!

ROSALIA: *(Blurting it out)* You threw your money to the four winds of heaven.

Domenica *(Severely)* And whose business was that, may I ask?

ROSALIA: *(Frightened, but unable not to drive her point home)* But, saints above—you never even noticed!

FILUMENA: *(With contempt)* Take no notice of him, it's no use.

DOMENICO: *(Controlling himself)* You're trying to provoke me, Filumena, you're going too far. Do you realize what you've done? You've made me look like a man of straw! Take these three young men I haven't even met, whose existence I hadn't even dreamed of, in fact—tomorrow or the next day, they can laugh in my face and say to themselves, "Fine, so that's Don Domenico. The man who foots the bill."

ROSALIA: *(Eagerly)* No, no, Don Mimi, what do they know about it? Donna Filumena, she does everything the right way, she has a head on her shoulders. It was the lawyer who sent the money when Michele— he's the engineer—set up shop in the next street. He told him it came from "a lady who wishes to remain anonymous!" *(She has difficulty with the last word.)* It was the same with Riccardo, he's the shirtmaker. And the lawyer has to send Umberto his monthly allowance, so he can finish up his studies. You don't come into it at all!

DOMENICO: *(Bitterly)* I only pay for it!

FILUMENA: *(On a sudden impulse)* I should have got rid of them, then? Is that what I should have done, Domenico? I should have put them out of the way, as other women do, is that what you mean? You'd admire a Filumena of that sort, wouldn't you? *(More excited)* Answer me! Tell me I should have done what the other girls said. "What are you waiting for?" they said, "it's one worry too many!" But I'd have worried to all eternity! How could I have lived with that on my conscience? And then, when I talked with the Madonna, the little Madonna at the end of our street... *(Turning to* ROSALIA*)* Remember?

ROSALIA: *(Almost insulted at the idea that she could forget)* Do I remember? It's the Madonna of the Roses! And does she shower her favors upon us? One a day!

FILUMENA: *(Re-creating the scene, as if talking to herself)* It was three o'clock in the morning. I was alone, walking down the street. Six months had passed since I left home. It was the first time. Where could I turn? Who could I confide in? I heard the other girls. "What are you waiting for?" "Just one worry too many." "I know a good one." Without knowing it, as I walked along, I'd come to "my" little street, with the little altar on the corner, the altar of the Madonna of the Roses. I went up to her. This way. *(She plants her fists on her hips and, raising her eyes to an imaginary effigy, speaks as one woman to another.)* "What am I to do? Thou who knowest all things, who knowest why I have sinned, tell me: what am I to do?" But the Madonna didn't reply. She didn't say a word. "So that's it?" I said. "The more you don't talk, the more people believe in you. But I'm speaking to you. *(Arrogantly)* Answer me!" And a voice answered me. It said: *(Now she imitates the tone of voice of someone not known to her; she hasn't been able to tell where the voice comes from.)* "A mother's a mother!" I froze. I was riveted to the spot—like this. *(She grows rigid and fixes her eyes on an imaginary effigy.)* If I'd turned around, maybe I'd have seen where the voice had come from, a house with a balcony, the next street, an open window… But then I said to myself, "Why at this particular moment? What do other people know of my affairs?" *(Pause)* Then…it was she, was it? It was the Madonna? I'd faced right up to her, so she agreed to talk? And of course, the Madonna makes use of us when she wants to talk… So when they said, "One worry too many," it was the Madonna speaking, the Madonna wanted to test me? *(Slowly)* I don't know if it was me, I don't know if it was the Madonna of the

Roses, who went like this *(She nods as if to say, "I have understood")* and said, "A mother's a mother," but I swore an oath. I swore to bring up my children. *(She turns to* DOMENICO.*)* And that's why I've been around you all these years! For their sake. For their sake I've put up with the way you've treated me, I've put up with...everything. And when that young fellow fell in love with me and wanted to marry me...remember? We'd been together five years then, you and I. At home you had your wife and out at San Potito you had me with three little rooms and a kitchen. It was the first apartment you found for me after you'd taken me out of the that place, four years after we first met. Well, this young fellow wanted to marry me. But you acted jealous. I can hear you now, "I'm married, I can't marry you. But if this other fellow marries you, I'll..." And you burst out crying. *You* can cry, even if *I* can't. You can cry all right. And I said to myself, "Go slow, Filumena, it can't be helped. Domenico loves you yet, just stick to San Potito and your three little rooms..." Two years later your wife died. Time passed. I was still at San Potito. I said to myself, "He's still young, he wouldn't want to tie himself to another woman for life, the day will come when he'll settle down, when he'll realize what sacrifices I've made..." So I waited. And sometimes I'd say, "Domenico, do you know who's just got married? The girl across the way. In the house with the little windows." And you'd smile, you'd burst out laughing, just like when you came to the...other place with your friends. Before San Potito. The wrong kind of laugh. I'd hear it on the stairs. It wasn't always the same man laughing, but it was always the same laugh. *(Bearing up)* I waited. I waited twenty-five years. Waited for Don Domenico's pleasure. He's an old man of fifty-two now, but that's nothing... *(With a change of tone, vehemently)* I could die with the shame of it! This old man of fifty-two thinks he's a schoolboy, runs after every skirt he sets eyes on, goes around with lipstick on my handkerchiefs, and installs in my house his latest little... *(Threatening)* Well, try it again, bring her to this house, now I'm your wife, I'll throw you out, both of you. We're married. Married by the holy priest. And this is my house!

(A bell rings offstage. ALFREDO leaves upstage right.)

DOMENICO: Your house! Ha! ha! ha! *(He laughs with forced irony.)* You make me laugh!

FILUMENA: *(Passionately)* All right, laugh! I don't mind hearing you laugh now. You wouldn't know how to laugh as you did then.

(ALFREDO returns. He gives everyone a good look. He's bothered by what he has to say.)

DOMENICO: *(Noticing him, ill-humoredly)* What do *you* want?

ALFREDO: Me? I just wanted to say they've brought that supper...

DOMENICO: Why in God's name do you all think I shouldn't eat?

ALFREDO: *(As much as to say: I wash my hands of this)* Very well, Don Domenico. *(Talking out through the door)* Come in!

(Two WAITERS from a restaurant come in with a wicker hamper and other supplies for a cold supper.)

FIRST WAITER: *(Rather unctuous and servile)* Your supper, signore! *(To his companion)* Put it here.

(SECOND WAITER puts the hamper down on the spot indicated.)

FIRST WAITER: Signore, I've only brought one chicken. It's such a big one. Enough for four, signore. All best quality goods! *(He starts opening up the supplies.)*

DOMENICO: (*Stopping him with a gesture, annoyed*) Do
you know what you can do? You can leave!

FIRST WAITER: Yes, signore, yes, indeed. (*Taking a
dessert out of the hamper and placing it on the table.*) This is
the dessert the young lady is so fond of. And this is the
wine...

(*There is silence all around. To remind* DOMENICO *of a
promise, he adopts a playful tone.*)

FIRST WAITER: You haven't forgotten, have you,
signore? Our little...

DOMENICO: What?

FIRST WAITER: You *have* forgotten? Well, signore, when
you came over to order the supper, don't you recall?
I asked if you happened to have any old clothes you
didn't need, and you said, "Come this evening, and if
things turn out the way I'm expecting, I'll have a brand
new suit. I'll make you a present of it."

(*The atmosphere is glacial. After a pause, in a tone
indicating ingenuous disappointment, the* FIRST WAITER
continues.)

FIRST WAITER: Things did *not* turn out the way you
wanted? (*He waits, but when* DOMENICO *still doesn't
answer, he is impatient.*) You didn't get the good news
you expected?

DOMENICO: (*Aggressively*) I told you to leave!

FIRST WAITER: (*Amazed at his reception*) We're going,
signore. Let's go, Carlo. The good news never came.
Just my luck.

(*The two* WAITERS *leave, upstage right.*)

FILUMENA: (*After a pause, ironically*) Eat, Don Mimì!
What's the matter with you? You're not eating? Have
you lost your appetite?

DOMENICO: *(Angry)* Sure, I'll eat. I'll eat *and* drink—
later on!

FILUMENA: When the corpse comes to keep you
company!

*(Enter DIANA by the main door. She is a good-looking girl
of twenty-two. That is, she tries to look twenty-two; actually
she's twenty-seven. She dresses rather snobbishly—with
affected elegance. She looks them all up and down. As she
enters, she is talking to everyone in general and no one in
particular. She evidently despises everybody. She doesn't
even notice FILUMENA's presence. She is carrying medicinal
packages, which she places on the table near the door. She
takes a nurse's white coat from a chair and puts it on.)*

DIANA: There was *such* a *mob* in the pharmacy, I just
couldn't get waited on, I had to go to another one,
couldn't get waited on there either, went from one
pharmacy to another, must have been to *eight* in all,
I'm sweating *all* over, Rosalia. *(In a bossy tone)* Do get
my bath ready, there's a good girl. Oh! *(Seeing the
roses)* roses, *red* roses, thank you, *thank* you, Domenico,
you're a *dear*, what an *odor*. I'm working up quite an
appetite, too. *(Picks up one of her packages)* I've found the
camphor…and the *adrenalin* but oxygen isn't to be had
for a *million* lire!

*(DOMENICO is fuming. FILUMENA isn't batting an eyelash,
she's just waiting. ROSALIA and ALFREDO seem pretty
amused and happy. DIANA lights a cigarette and sits by the
table, facing out front.)*

DIANA: I was just *thinking*, if she—heavens, how I *hate*
to say the word—but, here goes, if she *dies* tonight,
I'll leave, early in the morning. A girl friend of mine
has room for me in her car. I'd just be in the way here,
whereas at Bologna I've a *hundred and one* little things
to do! I'll be back in just about ten days, and we'll be

together again. Now tell me, how is she? Out of her
pain yet? Has the priest come?

FILUMENA: *(Controlling herself, with affected courtesy,
slowly approaching)* The priest has come.

*(DIANA is taken completely by surprise. She stands up and
backs away several paces.)*

FILUMENA: And seeing that I was on my deathbed...
(Breaking off) Take that coat off!

(Though almost stunned DIANA does as she is told.)

FILUMENA: Put it on that chair.

(DIANA does so.)

FILUMENA: Seeing that I was in extremis, the priest
advised Don Domenico Soriano to tie the bridal knot
with the good Lord's blessing.

*(Not knowing what attitude to take, and trying to find
something to do, DIANA takes one of the roses and raises it
to her nose. FILUMENA is furious and shouts harshly.)*

FILUMENA: PUT THAT ROSE DOWN!

*(DIANA puts the rose down like a German soldier obeying an
order. FILUMENA is polite again.)*

FILUMENA: Don Domenico found the priest's advice
good. He said to himself, "Fair enough: the poor
woman has stood by me for twenty-five years"—and
lots more that we haven't time or inclination to tell
you. He came to the bedside and we were married—
with two witnesses and the priest's blessing. Weddings
must do people a lot of good, signorina, this one
certainly did me. I felt better right away. I got up and
put off dying till another time. As for you, young lady,
you can't be a nurse where no one needs nursing!

*(FILUMENA sticks out the index finger of her right hand and
on every emphatic word strikes DIANA on the chin with it.
Each time DIANA shakes her head in an involuntary "No".)*

FILUMENA: And as for all those nasty goings-on, making love beside the deathbed and so forth, you better go and do it in someone else's house!

DIANA: *(Has now backed practically to the entrance with an idiotic smile on her face)* Yes, I see. Oh, yes!

FILUMENA: And if you can't think of a good place to go, you can go…can go…where I used to live…

DIANA: Where's that?

FILUMENA: Ask Don Domenico. He used to frequent such places. In fact he still does.

(DIANA, dominated by FILUMENA's vehement eye, almost mechanically:)

DIANA: Thank you. *(And she leaves, upstage right.)*

FILUMENA: Don't mention it. *(And takes up her position again at left.)*

DOMENICO: *(Who has been lost in his own thoughts, snaps back again)* So that's the way you treat her, is it?

FILUMENA: I treat her as she deserves.

DOMENICO: *(Taking up the thread of his previous argument)* You're a devil, Filumena, it isn't easy to deal with you. It isn't easy to understand what you say. But now I know you: you're like some poisonous moth—that destroys whatever it lights on. A short time ago you said something I've been thinking about. You said, "It's something else I want of you, and you'll give it to me!" It can't be money, you know I'd have given you money. *(He can't bear not knowing.)* What is it then? What are you holding back? What do you want of me? Speak!

FILUMENA: *(Simply)* A mother's a mother.

DOMENICO: What in heaven's name do you mean by that?

FILUMENA: Children should know who their mother is.

DOMENICO: So?

FILUMENA: *(Her heart overflowing now)* My children must know I'm their mother. They must know what I've done for them. I want them to love me. And they mustn't feel ashamed before other men, they mustn't be made to feel bad every time they fill out a blank!

DOMENICO: But why should they?

FILUMENA: Why should they? Why should they?! Don't you see, they've never had a family. And if you don't have a family, what's your family name? You can make one up, but what does it mean, with no relations to show, not even an uncle or an aunt? You have no name! But this is going to stop for my boys, Domenico, it's going to stop. You've given your name to *me*. Now I want it for my boys.

DOMENICO: My name?

FILUMENA: Your name's Soriano. Since this afternoon, *my* name's been Soriano, too. And now my children will be called Soriano.

(Pause)

DOMENICO: *(Swallowing the bitter pill)* I see. In fact I saw it coming. But I had to hear you actually say it. *(Now he is in a rage.)* You snake in the grass! *(Now he is shouting his head off.)* Adder, viper, cobra, python, boa constrictor! *(Lowering his voice a little)* And you want to bring your brood into my nest, do you? The house of the Sorianos is to be a house of another color, the son of the Sorianos'll play host to the sons of a…

FILUMENA: *(Has kept calm but has no intention of letting him say "prostitute" again)* The sons of…?

DOMENICO: The sons of Filumena Marturano. The sons of Filumena Marturano and I don't know who.

You don't know who. You thought you'd put your conscience to rest and live down your sinful past by presenting me with three strangers to live with! I'd die first! They will never set foot in this house! I swear by the sacred memory of my father...

FILUMENA: *(With a rush of genuine feeling and deep earnestness)* Don't swear! I swore an oath twenty-five years ago, and I've stuck to it. Don't swear an oath you wouldn't stick to. The day will come when you'll want something from me, Domenico, so don't go swearing you'll never accept it, don't swear that, Domenico, or you'll never forgive yourself!

DOMENICO: *(Overawed by* FILUMENA's *words, but angry)* What's in your mind now, you witch? I don't fear you, understand! I'm not afraid of *you!*

FILUMENA: Then why do you have to say so?

DOMENICO: Oh, be quiet! *(Taking off his house coat)* Alfredo, bring me my coat.

*(*ALFREDO *goes into the study.)*

DOMENICO: You'll leave tomorrow. This marriage is a clear case of fraud. I'll bring suit against you. I have witnesses, remember. *(He's working himself up again.)* And if I lose, I'll destroy you anyway, Filumena. I'll chop you up in little pieces!

FILUMENA: *(Ironically)* May I ask where you want to send me?

DOMENICO: *(Very far gone, and aggressive about it)* Back where you came from!

*(*ALFREDO *comes back with* DOMENICO's *coat.* DOMENICO *grabs it and puts it on.)*

DOMENICO: *(To* ALFREDO*)* Tomorrow morning you'll go for my lawyer: you know who that is?

*(*ALFREDO *nods. To* FILUMENA:*)*

DOMENICO: Then we'll talk.

FILUMENA: Then we'll talk.

DOMENICO: And bring your secret weapon, if you have one. You'll need it.

FILUMENA: I do have a secret weapon. I'll bring it.

DOMENICO: Well, a harlot's a harlot, Filumena Marturano! *(He leaves, laughing horribly, outrageously.)*

ROSALIA: You hear that laugh, Donna Filumena, you remember that horrible laugh? And what a horrible, nasty thing to say, too! *(She is weeping.)*

FILUMENA: *(Relaxing)* Sit down, Rosalia.

(As ROSALIA *sits at the opposite end of the table,* FILUMENA *realizes that the cold supper is before them.)*

FILUMENA: Our supper's all ready, you see.

*(*ROSALIA *dries her tears and begins to smile.)*

FILUMENA: And that wasn't what the voice said, it said: "A mother's a mother", Rosalia Solimene! *(She is enjoying the food.)*

END OF ACT ONE

ACT TWO

(The next day at nine in the morning. In order to clean the floor the maid has put all the chairs out of the way; some are on the terrace, others upside down on the table in DOMENICO's *study. The carpet, in the center of which stands the dining table, is folded back upon itself from all four sides. It is a fine, sunny morning.)*

*(*LUCIA, *the maid, is an agreeable, healthy girl of about twenty-three. She has completed the job, and is squeezing out her scrub mop in the bucket for the last time. Then she takes mop, stick, and bucket and puts them on the terrace. She starts setting the room to rights by turning down the four sides of the carpet.)*

ALFREDO: *(Comes in from the outer door, tired, sleepy)* Hi, Lucia.

LUCIA: *(Stopping him dead with the tone she uses—and the gesture)* Don't come walking on my floor with those feet of yours!

ALFREDO: *(Yawning)* All right, I'll walk on these hands of mine.

LUCIA: So that's your tune, is it? I've been sweating blood over this floor and…

ALFREDO: Tune, what tune? I—am—dead. Dead! Don Domenico kept me chasing around after him the whole night. Or sitting with him on the sea wall at Mergellina—which isn't the warmest place in the world. What made the Lord God send me to *him*? But I'm not grumbling. He's not treated me bad. No, I've seen life! Madonna! The times we had together! *(Enthusiastically)* May the Lord let him live to be a hundred, a thousand!... *(Misgiving strikes him.)* But— quietly, peacefully! I wasn't born yesterday. These all-night sessions are getting to be a bit much! *(He takes a chair and sits at the table—all of which is a preparation for a daring demand.)* Lucia, can I have some hot coffee?

LUCIA: *(Who has put the chairs back without paying attention to* ALFREDO's *outpouring)* No. There isn't any.

ALFREDO: *(Put out)* What d'you mean, there isn't any?

LUCIA: There isn't any. There were three cups. I drank one. Donna Rosalia didn't want the second one so I gave it to Donna Filumena. The third cup I'm keeping for Don Domenico—in case he comes back!

ALFREDO: *(Glaring and not convinced)* In case he comes back!

LUCIA: In case he comes back! Donna Rosalia hasn't made any coffee today.

ALFREDO: I suppose you couldn't make any youurself?

LUCIA: No, I couldn't. I don't even know how. Coffee's none of my business.

ALFREDO: Well, why didn't Donna Rosalia make any?

LUCIA: She went out. Early. She said she had to deliver three urgent letters. For Donna Filumena.

ALFREDO: *(Pricking up his ears)* Deliver three letters for Donna Filumena? *(About to repeat himself, shouting)* Deliver three let...

LUCIA: Deliver three letters for Donna Filumena.

ALFREDO: *(Deciding to remember his state of dire exhaustion)* Lucia, I *must* have some hot coffee!! Know what you can do, Lucia? Pour Don Domenico his cup of coffee. Pour it right now. Go on, fill the cup, fill it to the brim! Then take the cup between finger and thumb like this and—easy, easy—pour a drop, a little drop *(He makes the gesture of pouring quite a bit of coffee from one cup to another.)* into another cup that just happens to be standing by and feeling lonely! And don't you rob your master, Rosalia Solimene! Go to your kettle of lovely steaming water and fill up his cup!

LUCIA: *(Dryly)* And when he notices it?

ALFREDO: But he won't! His mind is on...higher things. Anyway, he may not come. *(He pulls himself together heroically.)* And age before beauty, my dear!

(LUCIA doesn't get this. So ALFREDO tries a simpler line.)

ALFREDO: I need it more than he does!

LUCIA: *(Submitting)* Well, let me go and heat it up for you.

(LUCIA is leaving left, but seeing ROSALIA enter right, she stops and tells ALFREDO.)

LUCIA: Here's Donna Rosalia. You still want this coffee?

ALFREDO: Donna Rosalia's here? Well, good: she can make Don Domenico some fresh coffee, can't she? Anyway, bring me that half cup.

(ROSALIA comes into the room. She sees ALFREDO but pretends not to. Full of her mission, she makes a beeline for FILUMENA's bedroom door.)

ALFREDO: *(ROSALIA's attitude not having escaped him, letting her get right to the door before he calls attention to himself.)* Rosalia, what is this? Have you lost your tongue?

ROSALIA: *(Indifferently)* Oh, I didn't see you.

ALFREDO: I'm the invisible man.

ROSALIA: Too bad. Little boys should be seen and not heard.

ALFREDO: *(Grandly ignoring this last)* You went out early this morning, didn't you?

ROSALIA: *(An enigma)* Did I?

ALFREDO: Where were you?

ROSALIA: I was at Holy Mass, if you must know, Mister Invisible Man!

ALFREDO: *(Incredulous)* At Holy Mass. *(Remembering)* You took Donna Filumena's three letters and placed them on the holy altar, I suppose?

ROSALIA: *(Trapped but controlling herself)* Why d'you ask—if you know?

ALFREDO: *(Also simulating indifference)* I was just wondering. *(Pause)* Who did you take them to?

ROSALIA: Some little boys like to be heard, don't they?

ALFREDO: *(This being too deep for him, he starts to bluster.)* Little boys? Little…

ROSALIA: You talk, Alfredo Amoroso, you talk a lot. What's more, you're a spy.

ALFREDO: *(Huffily)* And when did I ever spy on you, I'd like to know!

ROSALIA: Spy on me? What'd be the use of that? My record's as clear—as water from the crystal spring! What do I have to be ashamed of? *(She starts to reel off her life story: the singsong expression tells us she has done so very often before.)* Born in '70. Figure for yourself how many years I have to my name—of poor but honest parents, my mother Sofia Trombetta Solimene was a washerwoman, my father, Antonio Procopio Solimene was a blacksmith. Rosalia Solimene, myself in person, entered into the holy state of matrimony with Vincenzo

Bagliore, who could fix anything from an umbrella to a
fireplace, on the first day of April, 1887.

ALFREDO: All Fool's Day.

(ROSALIA *stopped cold, turns a little shrill.*)

ROSALIA: Did you say something?

ALFREDO: *(Very lah-di-dah)* Oh, no. *(With a gesture that
says, "Pray continue, my dear madam")* Go on!

ROSALIA: Three children were born of the union, three
children came into this world, and all at the same time.
When the midwife took the news to my husband, who
was at work in the very next street to ours, she found
him with his head in a bucket…

ALFREDO: Full of water from the crystal spring…

ROSALIA: *(Repeating her last phrase with severity)* With his
head in a bucket, due to a stroke—which brought him
down in sorrow to the grave. Bereft of my husband,
bereft of my parents every one…

ALFREDO: All three of them…

ROSALIA: *(As before)* My parents every one, and with
three children to raise, I came with the good Lord's
help to San Liborio Street—number eighty, and there
I made my living by selling flyswatters, alms boxes
and hats for the carnival at Piedigrotta, especially
flyswatters, which I manufactured myself, thus earning
the necessary cash for the upkeep of the family. Donna
Filumena lived at number seventy-nine. She was a little
girl then, she played with my three boys, but when
they were twenty-one they went away. They couldn't
find work here. One went to Australia, two went to
America. Haven't had word of them since. So here was
I—with my flyswatters and my paper hats, and I don't
wish to talk of it, or the blood rushes to my head, and
if by good fortune Donna Filumena hadn't taken me

on when Don Domenico came into the picture, I'd have ended up on the steps of a church, begging. *(Pause)*

ALFREDO: *(Sighing ironically)* I suppose I'll go down in sorrow to the grave not knowing *who* you gave those letters to.

ROSALIA: *(Stiffly)* The secret mission that has been entrusted to *me* cannot be made public at this time.

ALFREDO: *(Disappointed, and with the intensity of words carefully prepared)* You are not a nice woman, Rosalia Solimene, you aren't nice! You have a warped mind. And an ugly, evil face.

ROSALIA: *(Undismayed)* I'm not looking for a husband.

ALFREDO: *(As if nothing unpleasant had been said)* Now, how about sewing this button on for me? *(He shows her the place on his coat.)*

ROSALIA: *(Making for the bedroom, turning ever so slightly)* Tomorrow. If I have time.

ALFREDO: And you might put some new elastic in my shorts…

ROSALIA: Buy the elastic, and I'll put it in. Good-bye! *(Exits left, with dignity)*

(LUCIA enters upstage left. On a small plate she carries the half cup of coffee. But she is stopped in her tracks by the doorbell. She turns her back on ALFREDO and goes out right to answer the door. After a pause DOMENICO comes in, pale and sleepy, LUCIA behind him. He sees the coffee.)

DOMENICO: Is that coffee?

(LUCIA, looking meaningfully at ALFREDO, who has got up at the first sound of DOMENICO's voice:)

LUCIA: Yes, signore.

DOMENICO: Give it to me.

(LUCIA does so. DOMENICO drinks it right off.)

DOMENICO: Just what I needed.

ALFREDO: Just what *I* needed.

DOMENICO: *(To* LUCIA*)* Bring him a cup of coffee.

*(*DOMENICO *sits at the center table, covering his face in his hands, lost in his own thoughts.* LUCIA *is making signs to* ALFREDO *to tell him that the other half cup of coffee has already been diluted.)*

ALFREDO: *(Shouting out in impatience and anger)* Bring it all the same!

DOMENICO: What?

ALFREDO: *(With a forced smile)* She said the coffee's cold, and I said, bring it all the same.

DOMENICO: You went to the lawyer's?

ALFREDO: Yes.

DOMENICO: When's he coming?

ALFREDO: Whenever he can fit it in. Today for sure.

*(*LUCIA *comes in upstage left, carrying the full cup of diluted coffee. She gives it to* ALFREDO *and enjoys herself doing so. She leaves. Suspicious,* ALFREDO *goes through the motions of drinking.)*

DOMENICO: *(Continuing a thought aloud, with some fearfulness)* It's no good!

ALFREDO: *(Thinking he means this diluted coffee, but resigned)* No good at all, Don Mimi, I'll have to get some at a cafe when we go out...

DOMENICO: *(Disoriented)* Some what?

ALFREDO: *(With conviction)* Some coffee.

DOMENICO: What's coffee got to do with it? I was just saying that if the lawyer says I don't have a case, it's no good. I'm powerless.

ALFREDO: (*Is not listening. He is trying a sip of the coffee. He grimaces with disgust.*) No good? It's impossible!

DOMENICO: What do *you* know about it?

ALFREDO: (*A wise guy now*) What do *I* know? I know it turns my stomach!

DOMENICO: It makes *my* stomach turn! What a mess she's always made of things! She'll never make it!

ALFREDO: She doesn't know *how* to make it!

DOMENICO: So I'll take it to court, I'll take it to one court after another, I'll take it to the Supreme Court!

ALFREDO: (*Astonished, wondering if* DOMENICO *is crazy*) Heavens, Don Mimi, as God's above, all for one little cup of coffee?

DOMENICO: Cup of coffee? You idiot, I'm talking about Filumena…

ALFREDO: (*Groping*) Hm… (*Then it dawns.*) Ah!!! (*Then he is amused.*) Ha! Ha! (*But fearing* DOMENICO's *anger, he suppresses his laughter and becomes a model of gravity.*) Oh, yes, of course!

DOMENICO: (*Realizing what has been going on in* ALFREDO's *mind, accepts his incomprehension affectionately*) What's the use of talking about this with you? I could talk to you about the past, but this present business…? (*He looks at* ALFREDO *as if seeing him for the first time. He analyzes his present unhappy state.*) Look at him, what has he come to? White hair, drooping eyes, baggy cheeks! Alfredo Amoroso in his second childhood!

ALFREDO: (*Would never contradict his master, so he pleads guilty to all and resigns himself as to fate*) Dear God!

DOMENICO: (*Realizing that he himself has undergone changes*) Do you remember a certain Don Domenico Soriano, Don Mimi—do you remember him?

ALFREDO: *(His mind has been wandering and maybe he wouldn't have understood anyway)* Who's that? Who's dead? Don Domenico?...

DOMENICO: *(Swallowing the pill)* That's it, precisely: He's dead, Don Mimi Soriano is dead!

ALFREDO: *(Getting it now)* Oh, you mean...*you*, Don Mimi...you...good God!

DOMENICO: *(Seeing himself young in his mind's eye)* With black moustaches, thin as a rail, made night into day, never slept...

ALFREDO: *(Gaping)* You think I don't know?

DOMENICO: Remember that girl up on Capodimonte, that girl Gelsomina? She was terrific! "Let's elope, Mimi, *do* let's elope!" I can hear her voice still. Do you remember the vet's wife?

ALFREDO: Could I ever forget her? What a woman! Her sister-in-law was quite something too: what was her job? Wool carding. Ran after her a bit myself. Pity we weren't...er...what do you call it? Compatible? *(Enjoying the word)* We weren't compatible!

DOMENICO: You remember the old horse trail down to the villa? And me driving the best pair in Naples?

ALFREDO: You looked like a statue!

DOMENICO: Horses! Horses, buff and gray, *my* colors, my riding cap on my head, my whip in my hand, the finest horses in...remember Silver Eye?

ALFREDO: Unforgettable beast! *(Nostalgically)* Silver Eye the gray mare! She had a rump like a full moon! When you looked at that rump, you kept right on looking. It was the rising of the moon, the rising of the full moon. I fell in love with that horse. That's why I had to break off with the little wool carder. And when you sold her, oh! the soul of Alfredo Amoroso was grievous sick!

DOMENICO: Paris! London! I was God Almighty! I was master of my fate, not God Himself could change my place in the world, I was monarch of all I surveyed, king of the mountains, king of the seas, king of my own life. And now? Now, I'm through. No will, no enthusiasm, no passions, and if I do try anything, it's only to prove to myself that it isn't so, that I'm still strong, that I can still get the better of other men, that I can get the better of death itself. And I do so well I believe it! I convince myself, I surprise myself, and I go on fighting! You always have to go on fighting! Domenico Soriano never gives up and never gives in! *(Coming down to earth decisively)* Now what's been going on here? Have you found anything out?

ALFREDO: *(Tentatively)* Nothing for certain. They keep me in the dark. As I told you, Donna Filumena can't stand the sight of me. I don't know what I'm supposed to have done to her. As for Rosalia, Lucia tells me—and Rosalia confirms it—she's been delivering three urgent letters from Donna Filumena.

DOMENICO: *(To whom this precise number of letters seems not without significance)* To whom?

(FILUMENA *enters in her house dress, ungirt, followed by* ROSALIA, *who is carrying sheets and clean pillowcases. She notices the two men but pretends not to. She has heard their last words but ignores them. Concentrating on her work, she calls in the direction of the main door.)*

FILUMENA: Lucia! *(To* ROSALIA.) Give me the key.

ROSALIA: *(Offers her a bunch of keys)* Here you are.

FILUMENA: *(Pockets the keys)* Where is that girl? *(Shouts a bit louder)* Lucia!

LUCIA: *(Entering upstage left, hurriedly)* Yes, signora?

FILUMENA: *(Cutting her short)* Take these sheets.

(ROSALIA *consigns the sheets and pillowcases to* LUCIA.)

FILUMENA: In the little room next to the study, there's an ottoman, make it up as a bed...

LUCIA: Yes, signora.

*(*LUCIA *starts to go.* FILUMENA *stops her.)*

FILUMENA: Wait! I need your room, too. These are the clean sheets. You'll fix up a hammock in the kitchen.

LUCIA: *(Dismayed)* All right...but what about my things? Must I take them all out?

FILUMENA: I've told you: I need the room!

LUCIA: But where'm I to put my things?

FILUMENA: You can use the closet in the hall.

LUCIA: All right. *(She leaves upstage right.)*

FILUMENA: *(Pretending to be seeing* DOMENICO *for the first time)* You're here?

DOMENICO: *(Coldly)* May I ask what all these changes mean in my house?

FILUMENA: Certainly. There are no secrets between man and wife. I need two more bedrooms.

DOMENICO: You need...for whom?

FILUMENA: *(With precision)* For my sons. There should have been three of them, I know. But one's married, and they have four kids, so he's staying put.

DOMENICO: They have four kids, do they? And what's this tribe called, if I may ask?

FILUMENA: *(Still sure of her ground)* For the time being they have my name. Later on they'll have yours.

DOMENICO: *Not* without my consent.

FILUMENA: But you'll give your consent. *(Almost vengefully)* You'll give your consent, Domenico. *(She exits down right.)*

DOMENICO: *(Unable to control himself any longer)* I'll throw them out, understand? I'll *kick* them out!

FILUMENA: *(Offstage)* Close the door, will you, Rosalia?

(ROSALIA shuts the door in DOMENICO's face.)

LUCIA: *(Enters upstage right, turning to DOMENICO, quietly)* Signore, Signorina Diana is outside…with a man.

DOMENICO: *(Interested)* Show them in.

LUCIA: *(Who has obviously tried to show them in already)* She doesn't want to come in, signore. I said she should, but she said you should come outside to her… *(With conviction)* She's afraid of Donna Filumena.

DOMENICO: *(Put out)* Now look, *I* wear the pants in this house! Tell them to come in, tell them I am here!

(LUCIA leaves upstage right.)

ALFREDO: As soon as she sees her, she'll beat her to a pulp!

DOMENICO: *(Shouting so as to be heard on the other side of the closed door of the bedroom)* She will not. Alfredo, the time has come for me to make clear who is the master in this house! She is nothing: you can all put that in your pipe and smoke it.

LUCIA: *(Returning apologetically)* Signore, she won't come in. She says she can't answer for her nerves if she does.

DOMENICO: Who is it that's with her?

LUCIA: Just a man. I think she called him attorney somebody. *(Giving her private opinion)* If you ask me, he's scared, too!

DOMENICO: Ridiculous! There'll be three grown men here!…

ALFREDO: *(Earnestly)* Don't count me! In the state you've reduced me to I'm not worth a nickel. *(Firmly)* No, you can all have the discussion in here. I'll go wash my face in the kitchen. *(At the door)* When you want me, don't hesitate to call! *(He exits up left.)*

LUCIA: Well, signore, what's it to be?

DOMENICO: *(Swallowing)* I'll go out.

(LUCIA exits up left, DOMENICO up right. DOMENICO returns, bringing DIANA and attorney NOCELLA with him, insisting:)

DOMENICO: But good heavens, I tell you, this is my house and mine alone!

(DIANA, who has remained on the threshold with NOCELLA behind her, very excited:)

DIANA: Please, Domenico! After the scene of last night, I refuse to face that woman again!

DOMENICO: But, Diana, please, you're humiliating me. Come in, there's nothing to be afraid of!

DIANA: Afraid! *Me?* Why, I don't know what fear *is*! I simply can't be a party to *disgusting* behavior!

DOMENICO: Well, you won't be: / am here!

DIANA: You were here last night.

DOMENICO: Well, er, that was all…unexpected. Today, I assure you, you have nothing to fear. Come in. Attorney Nocella, do sit down.

DIANA: *(Taking several paces forward)* Where is she?

DOMENICO: I tell you again, don't worry. Just sit down, relax!

(They sit at the center table, DIANA to the left, NOCELLA in the middle, DOMENICO on the right, facing DIANA, who doesn't want to let the bedroom door get out of sight. She isn't at ease.)

DOMENICO: Now!

(NOCELLA *is a man of forty, average, rather a nonentity. Dresses with a certain sober elegance. He's discussing the Soriano case because* DIANA *has dragged him in here. His tone of voice indicates a certain lack of interest.*)

NOCELLA: I live in the same *pensione* as the signorina, that's where we got acquainted some time ago…

DIANA: Attorney Nocella can tell who I am, what sort of life I lead.

NOCELLA: *(Who doesn't want to get involved)* We see each other at table in the evening. Of course, I'm not in the *pensione* very much. I go to court, I see my clients, and then again I'm not much of a mixer…

DIANA: Domenico, would you mind *awfully* if we changed seats, *would* you? *(She wants a better view of the door, so they change.)* Now, last night, at table, I told this whole story of you and Filumena.

NOCELLA: That's right. We nearly laughed our heads off!

(DOMENICO *looks daggers at* NOCELLA.)

DIANA: Not at all. *I*, for one, *never* laughed!

(NOCELLA *is amazed but holds his tongue.*)

DOMENICO: *(Indicating* DIANA*)* She was here because I had her pretend to be a nurse.

DIANA: *(Up in arms)* Pretend, *pretend*! But, great heavens, I *am* a nurse! With diplomas and *everything*! Didn't I ever tell you, Domenico?

DOMENICO: No! Well, I mean…

DIANA: *(Interrupts him by clearing her throat loudly)* Well, of course, I didn't *have* to tell you, did I? The thing is, I've explained your position to Attorney Nocella, I've told him how you can't *bear* the idea of having to stay

tied to a woman you never chose to be tied to, and
Attorney Nocella has explained to me *at length…*

(A bell rings offstage.)

DOMENICO: *(Who hears it)* Excuse me, but I'll have to
ask you to go into my room. There's the bell.

(LUCIA crosses from left to right upstage.)

DIANA: *(Getting up)* Yes, I suppose we should.

(NOCELLA gets up, too.)

DOMENICO: *(Shows them into the study and follows)* Please
sit down.

NOCELLA: Thank you. *(Goes out first)*

DIANA: *(Following NOCELLA, whispers to DOMENICO)*
You're pale as a sheet!

(DIANA and DOMENICO leave.)

LUCIA: *(Brings UMBERTO in)* Sit down, please.

*(UMBERTO is a tall, well-built young man, dressed with
modest dignity, serious looking. He loves study. His way of
speaking, his sharp, observant eye, inspire respect.)*

UMBERTO: Thank you. *(He opens a notebook and makes
some corrections in pencil.)*

LUCIA: Won't you sit down. Donna Filumena may be a
few minutes yet.

UMBERTO: I'd like to. Thanks.

*(UMBERTO sits on the left, by the terrace. The bell rings
again. LUCIA goes to answer it. Pause. Then she reenters
with RICCARDO.)*

LUCIA: Come in here, please.

*(RICCARDO is likable, lithe, lively, with very mobile black
eyes. Dressed with rather showy elegance. Looks at his
wristwatch as he enters. LUCIA starts to go down left.)*

RICCARDO: Hey! One moment.

(LUCIA *turns back.*)

RICCARDO: How long have *you* been here?

LUCIA: Eighteen months.

RICCARDO: *(Quite a lad)* You're a damn good-looking girl, you know.

LUCIA: *(Flattered)* But I'll spoil with time!

RICCARDO: Why not stop by at my store some day…

LUCIA: You have a store?

RICCARDO: Number seventy-four, Via Chiaia, next to the porter's lodge. I'm a shirtmaker.

LUCIA: Really? And what would I do with a man's shirt? Get along with you!

RICCARDO: I take care of men *and* women. I put the men's shirts on, and I take the women's shirts off! *(With this last pronouncement* RICCARDO *embraces* LUCIA *fervently.)*

LUCIA: *(Disentangling herself, offended)* Hey, stop it! *(She frees herself.)* Are you crazy? What do you take me for? I'll tell the signora!

(LUCIA, *thinking of* UMBERTO *who, however, isn't interested:)*

LUCIA: And with him in the room!

(The bell rings. LUCIA *starts to go.)*

RICCARDO: *(Noticing* UMBERTO *for the first time, amused)* Why, look! And I never even saw him!

LUCIA: *(Right back at him)* You don't see much. Except bad women…

RICCARDO: *(With an insinuation)* You'll come to the store?

LUCIA: *(Holding her ground)* Number seventy-four? *(Looking at him admiringly)* Via Chiaia?

(LUCIA, *at a sign from* RICCARDO *meaning "yes":*)

LUCIA: I'll be there. *(She exits upstage right. In the doorway she throws him a meaningful smile.)*

RICCARDO: *(Walks up and down a little. A couple of times his eyes meet* UMBERTO's. *He is slightly uncomfortable.)* Nice girl. *(Pause)* Don't you think so?

UMBERTO: It's all one to me.

RICCARDO: How's that? Studying to be a priest?

*(*UMBERTO *pays no attention to him. Goes on writing.)*

LUCIA: *(Bringing in* MICHELE*)* Step this way, please.

*(*MICHELE *is dressed in his blue plumber's overalls. He carries a bag of tools. In good health, flourishing, rather fat. He takes off his beret as he comes in.)*

MICHELE: What goes on here, Lucia? Is it that bathroom faucet again? I thought I soldered it good.

LUCIA: No, it's working.

MICHELE: Then what is it this time?

LUCIA: Nothing, nothing at all. The faucets are fine. Just wait while I call Donna Filumena. *(She exits down left.)*

MICHELE: *(Speaks deferentially to* RICCARDO*)* Good morning, sir.

*(*RICCARDO *nods curtly.)*

MICHELE: There's nobody to mind the shop!

*(*RICCARDO *gives him another look.* MICHELE *consents to be more explanatory.)*

MICHELE: I mean, I hope she'll come soon. *(He takes a cigarette butt out of his pocket.)* Anyone got a light?

RICCARDO: *(Haughtily)* Sorry, no.

MICHELE: Smoking strictly prohibited. *(Awkward pause)* You're a relative?

RICCARDO: Is this a court of inquiry?

MICHELE: How d'you mean?

RICCARDO: My friend, I can see you're crazy about discussions. I'm not.

MICHELE: You should remember your manners, *you* should!

UMBERTO: *(Intervening)* He forgot them years ago.

RICCARDO: Now look here...

UMBERTO: Excuse me, you come in here as if you owned the place, you throw your arms around the housemaid, while doing so you see me, and aren't in the least embarrassed, and now you spit on this poor creature.

MICHELE: *(Coming right back at* UMBERTO*)* Poor creature, am I? If anyone spits on me, *he'll* get an eyeful! *(Turning to* RICCARDO.*)* You can thank your stars we're indoors.

RICCARDO: You *annoy* me, understand? Indoors or out!

MICHELE: *(Puts his tool bag down, turning pale)* Let's see then!

*(*MICHELE *comes slowly toward* RICCARDO.*)*

RICCARDO: *(Comes toward him with the same stealth)* Sure, let's see!

*(*UMBERTO *now tries to intervene. He aims at stopping either of them taking the initiative.)*

MICHELE: *(Angry at* UMBERTO*)* You little sonofa...

*(*MICHELE *aims a blow at* UMBERTO, *but the latter, too quick for him, only receives half its force.)*

MICHELE: You get out of the way!

(Now there's a real scuffle at close quarters with many blows and kicks that miss their mark and with words, or rather half-words, spoken in rage between clenched teeth.)

FILUMENA: *(Comes in from down left, her tone brisk)* What's going on here?

(ROSALIA follows at her heels.)

(The three sons pull out of the scrimmage at the first sound of FILUMENA's voice. They are now ranged in front of her trying to look as if nothing had happened.)

FILUMENA: Now, where do you all think you are?

UMBERTO: *(Rubbing a sore nose)* I was trying to keep them apart.

RICCARDO: So was I.

MICHELE: Me, too.

FILUMENA: So who was doing the fighting?

MICHELE, RICCARDO & UMBERTO: *(In unison)* Not me!

FILUMENA: You ought to be ashamed. *(Pause. She has momentarily lost her briskness. Is at a loss)* Boys, I, er… *(Trying again)* well, how *is* everything?

(There is another slight pause till MICHELE decides to be the first to speak up.)

MICHELE: I've nothing to gripe about—thanks be to God.

FILUMENA: How are the children?

MICHELE: Pretty good. Last week the middle one had a bit of fever, now he's okay. He ate four pounds of grapes. Mamma wasn't looking, I wasn't home, his tummy was like a big drum, but you know how it is with four kids. If it isn't one, it's the other, there's always something. Take the way all of mine like castor oil. When we give it to one of them, the other three shout the house down till we give it to them too. Two hours later there they all are on their little pots—in a row!

UMBERTO: *(Breaking up this low conversation)* I got your note, signora. I'm afraid your name didn't mean a thing to me. It was the address that started me thinking. I realized that this Donna Filumena was someone I see nearly every evening on my way to the newspaper office. One time I even walked her home—to this address—she had a sore foot and couldn't walk properly. It was a pleasure to help her… *(Drawing breath for an eloquent paragraph)* My reconstruction of the story…

FILUMENA: I had a sore foot, that's right.

RICCARDO: *(To bring things to a point)* Now what's it all about?

FILUMENA: *(To* RICCARDO*)* How's the store doing?

RICCARDO: Fine, why shouldn't it? Though if all my customers were like you, I'd have to shut up shop in a month. Excuse my frankness, signora, but when *you* come there, I feel like running for cover. You give me such a time. You make me unpack every piece of merchandise in the place. "No, not this, I'll take that, no, not that, I must think it over!" And you leave the store in such a mess it'd take a staff of fifty to put it straight.

FILUMENA: *(Maternally)* I simply mustn't trouble you in future, must I?

RICCARDO: *(Taken aback)* I don't mean that, signora! The customer's the boss, after all. I just meant I can only sweat through one shirt at a time.

FILUMENA: *(At ease now)* Well, now, I've called you all together for a serious reason. If you'll step in here *(Pointing to her bedroom)* for a moment, we can talk it over…

(DOMENICO *comes in from the study followed by* NOCELLA. *He again speaks in his normal tone, that of a man who is sure of himself. He turns to* FILUMENA *with good-natured energy:)*

DOMENICO: That won't be necessary, Filumena, let's not mix things up even worse than they are already. *(To* NOCELLA*)* I'm no lawyer, but I said it would be this way. I thought of it before you did, it was as plain to me as the nose on your face! *(To* FILUMENA, *who is looking doubtingly at* NOCELLA.*)* This is Attorney Nocella. He's going to clarify this whole situation. *(To the three sons.)* The signora made a mistake. She has brought you here for nothing. You may go—we're sorry for the inconvenience.

FILUMENA: Just a moment! I made no mistake, sending for these boys, and what business is it of yours anyway?

DOMENICO: *(Meaningfully)* You think we can say it all before strangers?

FILUMENA: *(Grasps the fact that somehow the whole course of things has changed,* DOMENICO's *tone makes this unmistakable. She turns to the three boys)* Will you be patient for another five minutes, boys? Wait for me on the terrace, will you?

(UMBERTO *and* MICHELE *start off in that direction with a little hesitation.)*

RICCARDO: *(Looking at his watch)* Listen, signora. I think you take advantage of people. I've got things to do…

FILUMENA: *(Losing her temper)* Didn't I say there was a serious reason? *(Treating him as a little boy, in a tone that admits of no reply.)* Go out on the terrace. The others are waiting, you'll wait too!

RICCARDO: *(Disconcerted by her firmness)* Well, all right.

(RICCARDO *will leave with the other two.)*

FILUMENA: *(To* ROSALIA*)* Give them some coffee, Rosalia.

ROSALIA: Yes, Donna Filumena. *(To the three of them)* Go out on the balcony and sit down *(Showing them where to sit.)* And I'll be right out with some lovely coffee!

(ROSALIA *exits upstage left, while the boys go out on the terrace.)*

FILUMENA: Well?

DOMENICO: *(Loftily)* This gentleman is a lawyer. Suppose you talk to *him.*

FILUMENA: *(Impatiently)* What good ever came of the law?

(DOMENICO *clears his throat audibly.)*

FILUMENA: Well, what is it?

NOCELLA: It's like this, signora, as I said, this…er… situation is no business of mine…

FILUMENA: Then what d'you want?

NOCELLA: That's just it. It's no business of mine in the sense that this gentleman isn't my client, nor has he summoned me…

FILUMENA: Were you sent? Or did you just come?

NOCELLA: Well, now, signora, I could *never* permit myself to be *sent…*

DOMENICO: *(To* FILUMENA*)* For God's sake, let him speak!

NOCELLA: The signorina told me about the case. *(Looking back toward the study)* Where is she?

DOMENICO: *(Rather irritated, and trying to bring the discussion back on the rails)* Attorney Nocella, I think, well, who told you is beside the point. State your conclusions.

FILUMENA: *(Looking toward the study)* She's in there, is she, she just hasn't the courage to show herself! Go on, Mister Lawyer!

NOCELLA: In the situation described by this gentleman...no, by the young lady...

*(*DOMENICO *coughs peremptorily.)*

NOCELLA: ...dealing with cases of this sort...well, I've found a CLAUSE. *(He is a drowning man, the clause is a straw.)* Clause Number 101! *(He takes a paper from his pocket.)* "Matrimony under imminent peril of death." *(Starting to reel it off)* "In the case of imminent peril of death..."

(Another cough from DOMENICO *stops* NOCELLA.)*

NOCELLA: It explains all the different possibilities. But then this was *not* a case of imminent peril of death— because your imminent peril was peril pretended or peril feigned, that comes under another heading...

DOMENICO: I have witnesses: Alfredo, Lucia, the janitor, Rosalia...

FILUMENA: The nurse.

DOMENICO: The nurse. All of them. No sooner was the priest out of the room than she bounced out of bed and shouted, "We're man and wife, Domenico Soriano!"

NOCELLA: So the clause we want is Number 122: "Violence and error." *(He digs another paper out of his pocket and reads.)* "The validity of a marriage may be impugned by one or other of the parties if his or her consent has been extorted by violence or granted in error." The consent of this gentleman, having been granted in error, I submit, on the basis of Clause 122, that the validity of this marriage...

FILUMENA: Attorney Nocella, I don't know what you're talking about.

DOMENICO: *(Confident that he has understood)* Don't you see? I married you because you were about to die…

NOCELLA: No! Matrimony is unconditional! Clause 164. *(He recites by heart this time.)* "Should the aforesaid parties add, spend, or otherwise affix restrictions, qualifications, modifications, or other conditions, no priest of the church, no official of the state may proceed to the celebration of matrimony."

DOMENICO: But you said, if there was no imminent peril of death…

FILUMENA: Be quiet, you don't understand it any more than I do. Mister Lawyer, explain it to us.

NOCELLA: *(Offering her the papers)* Read it for yourself.

FILUMENA: *(After a moment's hesitation, takes the paper and tears it very deliberately in two. Her voice is low.)* What use is paper to me? The likes of Filumena Marturano can't read, Mister Lawyer!

NOCELLA: *(Roused)* Signora, since you were *not* dying, your marriage is annulled, your marriage is not valid.

FILUMENA: What about the priest?

NOCELLA: The priest says it was a desecration of the Sacrament. The marriage is not valid.

FILUMENA: *(Livid)* Not valid! I had to die?

NOCELLA: Exactly.

FILUMENA: If I *had* died…

NOCELLA: The marriage would have been valid.

FILUMENA: And he could have married again, he could have had children?

NOCELLA: Naturally. This hypothetical wife would have been marrying the deceased Signora Soriano's widower.

DOMENICO: You *would* have been Signora Soriano...but dead.

FILUMENA: The idea appeals to you, doesn't it? *(Changing her tone)* All I've ever wanted is a family. I spend a lifetime at it, and now the law says "no". Is that justice, Mister Lawyer?

NOCELLA: The law, my dear signora, cannot uphold *your* principles—however human they may be—if it thereby becomes accessory to measures operating to the detriment of a third person. Domenico Soriano has no intention of marrying you.

DOMENICO: And if you don't believe Attorney Nocella, consult any lawyer you do believe.

FILUMENA: I believe him. Not because you say the same thing—you have your own fish to fry. Not because *he's* a lawyer, I don't know lawyers. I believe him because you can look me in the face. D'you think I don't know you by this time? Why, you're your old self again, you're cocky, you're the boss, when I look at you, you look right back. That means you're telling the truth, Domenico. When you tell a lie, you don't know *where* to look, you start looking for flies on the ceiling!

DOMENICO: Attorney Nocella, proceed.

NOCELLA: As you wish, Signor Soriano.

FILUMENA: *(Is still pondering the lawyer's sentence, "Domenico Soriano has no intention of marrying you". Through the following speech she becomes more and more wrought up.)* Domenico Soriano has no intention of marrying me. I've no intention of marrying him either. I don't want you. Go on, Mister Lawyer, I don't want him anymore! It's not true I was dying, I admit it, I just wanted to cheat him. I'd stolen from him before, and now I wanted to steal—a name, a family name! But, as for the law, there's the sort of law that makes people cry, isn't there, Mister Lawyer? I want you to know there's another law—that makes people *laugh*— and that's the law for me! *(In the hard tone of ACT ONE)* You boys, come in now!

DOMENICO: *(Who'd like to smooth things over)* Filumena, stop!

FILUMENA: *(Violently)* You be quiet!

(The three sons come in from the balcony, rather disoriented, and take up their positions in the center of the stage. ROSALIA comes in upstage left with the coffee. She sees that this isn't the right moment and puts her tray on a sideboard. She listens. She gets gradually nearer FILUMENA down the left side of the stage. Now the stage is set. FILUMENA continues.)

FILUMENA: Now listen to what I have to say. *(Indicating DOMENICO and NOCELLA)* That's people, that's the world. The world with its rights of men, and laws, and clauses, the world that defends itself with pen and paper: Attorney Nocella and Don Domenico Soriano. *(Striking herself on the chest)* And I am Filumena Marturano. A woman who doesn't know the law. A woman who wants a law of her own. A woman who can't cry. You see my eyes, how dry they are? Like tinder. *(Looking straight at the three boys)* I am your mother.

DOMENICO: Filumena!

FILUMENA: *(Grimly)* Who are you to stop me telling them? *(To NOCELLA)* Can I tell 'em or not? What does the law say to that? *(More aggressively than emotionally)* You are my children. I am Filumena Marturano— there's no need to explain that name, young fellows like you will have heard of me.

(They are petrified.)

FILUMENA: I have nothing to say of Filumena
Marturano. But I remember a girl of seventeen… *(Her
mind fills with memories. Pause)* Do you know the slums
of Naples, Mister Lawyer? San Giovaniello, Vergini,
Forcella, Tribunale, Pallonetto. Do you know the
smoke, the blackness? In summer you can't breathe
for the heat, there are too many people. In winter the
cold makes your teeth chatter. The narrow streets
swarming with grimy children, the hovels they live in,
dark even at noon. In one of those ratholes, San Liborio
Street, lived the Marturanos, a mob of Marturanos.
What became of them all later, what the end was, I
don't know, I don't want to know. But I can see us as
we were then, I can see the sullen faces, the crowded
beds. We went to sleep without a good night, we got
up without a good morning. I can only remember one
thing my father ever said, and I wish I could forget
that. I was thirteen, and he said, "You're a big girl now:
do you know there's nothing to eat?" How hot it was!
You could hardly breathe! I can see us sitting around
the table every evening. The table had one large dish
on it and forks all around, nothing but forks. There was
no pleasure at those meals. If I dropped my fork, I felt
I'd been caught stealing. *(Pause)* I don't know when I
found out that some people aren't poor. I used to stand
on the corner of some big street downtown and look
at all the people with good shoes on, good clothes, and
the good girls on the arm of their good husbands-to-
be. One evening—when I was seventeen—I saw a girl
I knew. I hardly recognized her, she was so dressed
up—though maybe any decent clothes seemed dressy
to me at that time. She told me things. *(Pause)* I didn't
close my eyes all night. How hot it was! *(Abruptly)*
That's how I got to know you. There. Remember?
Maybe you didn't think much of the place—to me it
was a palace. One evening I went to see the family on
Liborio Street. I was all of a tremble. I said to myself:

"They won't look me in the face, they'll throw me out!" No one said a thing. Someone offered me a chair. Someone even stroked my cheek. I was a visitor from the great world, so they scraped the floor before me. Only my mother…well, when I went over to say good-bye, there were tears in her eyes. That was Filumena's last homecoming. *(Pause)* Not a pretty story, is it? All I'll say for myself is this: I didn't murder my children. For twenty-five years I've thought of nothing else. My family! *(If there's a light in her eyes at this moment, she comes down to earth at once and addresses herself directly to the three boys.)* And here you are! I've raised you, I've made men of you, I've stolen from him *(Indicating* DOMENICO*)* to bring you up…

MICHELE: *(Comes over to* FILUMENA*, full of emotion)* All right, all right, that's enough… *(He is almost too moved to speak.)* What more could you have done?

UMBERTO: *(Also coming over, gravely)* There are so many things I wish I could say. I'm not much good at talking, though. I'll write you a letter.

FILUMENA: *(Simply)* I don't know how to read.

UMBERTO: *(Quietly)* I'll read it to you.

(Pause. FILUMENA *waits for her third son to come over, but* RICCARDO *goes out through the door without a word.)*

FILUMENA: *(After a pause)* He's gone.

UMBERTO: *(With sympathy)* Oh, that's just him. He didn't understand. Tomorrow I'll stop by and talk to him.

MICHELE: You can come with me, signora. It's a small place, but there's a room. There's a terrace. *(Cheerfully)* The kids are always asking me, "Where's granny? Where's granny?" And I always have to make something up! Now I'll go home and say, "She's here!"

and it'll be like the carnival of Piedigrotta. *(Urging her)* Let's be going!

FILUMENA: *(Firmly)* Yes. I'll come.

MICHELE: Fine, let's go then.

FILUMENA: Just a moment. Wait for me at the gate *(To* UMBERTO*)* You can go down together. I need ten minutes—to tell Domenico something.

MICHELE: *(Happily)* Good, I'll do that. *(To* UMBERTO*)* You're coming?

UMBERTO: Sure I'll come with you.

MICHELE: Good-bye, everybody! *(To* UMBERTO*)* I could tell there was something, that's why I wanted to talk!

(They leave.)

FILUMENA: Mister Lawyer, *(She points to the study.)* give us two minutes.

NOCELLA: No, I think I'll be leaving.

FILUMENA: No, no, just two minutes, you should be here when I'm through talking to Don Domenico. Go and sit down.

(NOCELLA reluctantly goes into the study. Without a word, ROSALIA exits down left.)

FILUMENA: *(After a pause, calmly)* I'm going, Domenico. Tell the lawyer to do whatever a lawyer does. I deny nothing. I leave you free.

DOMENICO: I should think so. You could have just asked for money instead of making all this song and dance.

FILUMENA: *(Still very calm)* Tomorrow I'll send for my things.

DOMENICO: You're crazy, if you ask me. What do you want to do to those three boys? Destroy their peace of mind? Who put you up to it? *Why* did you say that?

(Pause)

FILUMENA: *(Coldly)* Because one of those three boys is your son.

*(*DOMENICO *turns to stone. A long pause)*

DOMENICO: Do you know what you're saying?

FILUMENA: *(Without change in manner)* One of those three boys is your son.

DOMENICO: *(Not daring to shout. Intensely)* Quiet!

FILUMENA: I could have said they were all your sons, you'd have believed it, I'd have made you believe it, but it isn't so. I know what you're thinking, you're thinking I could have told you. But I couldn't. Because you wouldn't have treated the other two right. Men are all alike, Domenico, and children are all alike. Children are created equal, too.

DOMENICO: You're lying!

FILUMENA: No, Domenico, no! Let me remind you. You can't remember because you were always going off… London, Paris…the races…other women… Let me remind you. Remember how much you paid me? You used to leave a hundred lire bill on the dressing table. Do you remember the night you said to me, "Filumena, we love each other", just before you put the light out? You didn't love me, Domenico, but I loved you. You were joking, and when you switched the light on again, you gave me the usual hundred lire bill. I put the date on it—I know numbers even if I don't know writing. Then you went on another trip. I waited. Like Our Lady of the Sorrows. You don't remember what happened, I didn't tell you, I told you my life was still the same, and it was true: when I saw you hadn't understood, I went back to—the old life.

DOMENICO: *(Half to himself, slightly less convinced)* It isn't true.

FILUMENA: Domenico, I swear it by the Madonna of the Roses!

DOMENICO: *(Believing without hesitation)* Ah! *(Pause)* Which one is it, then?

FILUMENA: *(Firmly)* I won't tell. *(Trying to smile it off)* Men are created equal.

DOMENICO: *(After a short pause, firmly)* You're lying, the whole story is a lie! You'd have told me at the time, so you could keep me, so you could hold me in the hollow of your hand. You'd have told me at the time. *That* would have been a secret weapon, Filumena Marturano, and you want me to believe you wouldn't have used it?

FILUMENA: I wouldn't have used it. Because you wouldn't have let my children live. I thought that then, and I think it now. You'd have had me murder them, Domenico, so I didn't dare tell you. But for me your son would be dead.

DOMENICO: Which of them is he?

FILUMENA: Children are created equal.

DOMENICO: *(At his wits' end, nasty)* They're equal all right—your children. I don't want to see them. Get out! I don't know them. I don't know—my son.

FILUMENA: Yesterday I said, "The day will come when you'll want something from me, so don't go swearing you'll never accept it". Remember? Now you know *why* I said it. Good-bye, Domenico. But let me promise you one thing: If you tell my children what I've told you, I'll kill you. And I don't just talk about killing the way you do. A promise is a promise to Filumena Marturano. *(She breaks off. Calls briskly in the direction of the study)* Mister Lawyer! Come out of hiding, I won't hurt you. You've won your point, and I'm going. *(In the*

direction of the bedroom) Rosalia! I'm going. Tomorrow
I'll send someone for my things.

(NOCELLA *comes out of the study followed by* DIANA.
From the left comes ROSALIA *and from upstage right comes*
ALFREDO.)

FILUMENA: Good luck to you all! Patience, Rosalia!
Good-bye to you, Mister Lawyer! And no ill feelings!
(To DOMENICO, *good-humoredly.)* You've understood,
haven't you, Domenico? I'll say it again in front of
everyone: what I've told you is a secret. Tell nobody
nothing. *(She takes a locket from her breast, opens it, and
takes out a hundred lire bill, folded very small. She tears a
piece off and puts it back in the locket.)* Here's a hundred
lire bill. I'm tearing off one corner, there's something
written on it that I may need one day. *(Throwing the
bill in* DOMENICO's *face.)* The hundred lire are for you, I
hope you'll find it useful—even if you can't buy a son
with it, Domenico Soriano!

END OF ACT TWO

ACT THREE

(Ten months later. Flowers everywhere. Many of them in beautifully arranged baskets with the donors' names sticking out on cards. The flowers are of delicate shades: not red, but not white either. The whole house breathes an atmosphere of festivity. The curtains between the dining room and the study are closed. It is almost evening.)

(ROSALIA enters in her best black silks from upstage right. At the same time DOMENICO comes in from the study: he is wearing a smart blue suit. This man has undergone a complete change. There is no sign now—in gesture or tone of voice—of his old domineering nature. He has become mild and humble. His hair is a shade whiter, too. ROSALIA is moving across down left when he stops her.)

DOMENICO: You've been out already, Rosalia?

ROSALIA: I've been doing an errand for Donna Filumena.

DOMENICO: What errand's that?

ROSALIA: *(With good-natured insinuation)* Are you jealous, Don Domenico? I've been to San Liborio Street.

DOMENICO: San Liborio Street? What for?

ROSALIA: *(Playfully)* Ah! So he *is* jealous!

DOMENICO: *(With quiet irony)* Terribly jealous, I've noticed it myself.

ROSALIA: *(Not wishing to needle him)* Nonsense, it's just old Rosalia's little joke. *(Looking apprehensively toward* FILUMENA'*s room)* I'll tell you, but you mustn't tell Donna Filumena I've told you, she doesn't want you to know…

DOMENICO: Then don't tell me!

ROSALIA: Silly man! I'm doing a good deed, telling you, it's something that does Donna Filumena credit. *(Then in a dramatic whisper)* She had me carry a thousand lire and fifty candles to the Madonna of the Roses in San Liborio Street. *(Becoming more explanatory)* You know the old crone who lives on the corner and looks after the lamp and the flowers and everything? I had to go to her and say, "Donna Filumena wants you to light these candles at six this evening—on the nose!"

DOMENICO: Six o'clock on the nose?

ROSALIA: Don't you know the time of your own wedding, Don Domenico? At six o'clock on the nose, you and Donna Filumena will be man and wife. Good and proper this time. And while you're getting married in here, the candles will be lit in San Liborio Street at the feet of the Madonna of the Roses.

DOMENICO: I see.

ROSALIA: You're marrying an angel from heaven, Don Domè. A young girl of an angel, too. She gets younger and lovelier every day. I knew everything was all right. "You think Don Domenico'll forget you?" I said to her. "Him getting the marriage annulled, that was just one of his tantrums, the marriage bells haven't stopped ringing for *you*, Donna Filu…"

DOMENICO: That will do, Rosalia. Now suppose you go to your mistress.

ROSALIA: I'm going, I'm going. *(But she can't be hustled.)* You're marrying an angel from heaven. If it wasn't

for her, I'd have come to a bad end. She took me in,
and here I stayed, and here I am, and here I shall die. I
have everything ready for the day, a lovely long white
shirt with a fine piece of lace to it, white stockings, nice
underclothes, a bonnet on my head, I have it all ready
in the oak chest, and Donna Filumena knows about it,
too, she's going to lay me out herself, she's all I have,
of course my boys may come back, where there's life
there's hope... *(Checking herself with a big sniff)* You
don't mind if I leave now, do you, Don Domè? *(Exits
down left.)*

(Alone, DOMENICO *walks around the room a little, looking
at the flowers, reading the cards. Then he involuntarily
completes his thoughts aloud.)*

DOMENICO: Well, this is it!

(From upstage right are heard the voices of the three sons.)

MICHELE: Six o'clock, the ceremony is at six o'clock.

RICCARDO: But you were supposed to be there before...

UMBERTO: *I* was on time anyway!

(They enter.)

MICHELE: I guess we said five, but I was only three
quarters of an hour late.

RICCARDO: And you didn't let us know.

MICHELE: Now look. When you say meet me at five,
that means sort of *around* five, and what's around five?
Five-twenty, five-thirty, quarter of six...

RICCARDO: A quarter past eight the morning after, the
following month, two years later...

MICHELE: Oh, come on. It's like this. We got a clock as a
wedding present. But how long d'you suppose it lasted
when the first kid started walking?

UMBERTO: *(Seeing Don* DOMENICO*)* Hello—Don Domenico.

RICCARDO: *(Greeting him in the same deferential way)* Don Domenico.

MICHELE: Don Domenico.

(They are again ranged across the center of the stage, silent.)

DOMENICO: Hello to you! *(Long pause)* Well? Why've you stopped talking? You were discussing…

UMBERTO: *(Confused)* Yes, that's right…

RICCARDO: *(Starting off confidently but collapsing)* Why, sure, we were just saying…just saying…

MICHELE: *(Cheerfully)* Well, you have to stop talking sometime!

DOMENICO: As soon as you see me, in fact. *(To* MICHELE*)* You were late for your appointment?

MICHELE: Yes, sir, Don Domenico.

DOMENICO: *(To* RICCARDO*)* But you were on time?

RICCARDO: Yes, sir, Don Domenico.

DOMENICO: *(To* UMBERTO*)* How about you?

UMBERTO: Right on time, Don Domenico.

(Pause)

DOMENICO: Well, sit down anyway.

(They sit facing him.)

DOMENICO: The ceremony is at six. *(Pause)* So there's time. *(Pause)* At six the priest will be here. *(Pause)* No guests, just ourselves, that's how Filumena wanted it. *(Pause)* I just want to tell you… *(Pause)* I think I even did tell you once before… *(Pause)* This "Don Domenico" stuff isn't…right.

UMBERTO: *(Tentatively)* No—it isn't.

MICHELE: It isn't right at all.

UMBERTO: But...er...you haven't said...what you want us to call you.

DOMENICO: Well, you see, I couldn't help hoping— you'd come to your own conclusions. This evening I'm marrying your mother. And as for...the part of it that concerns you, I've been to my lawyer about it, and by tomorrow you'll all be called Soriano.

(The three of them look at each other to decide who should speak first.)

UMBERTO: *(Plucking up courage)* Well, you see...I know I can answer for the three of us, we all feel the same way. *(Bracing himself for a statement)* We're not children, we're men, so it isn't easy for us to...er...call you... what you wish to be called, generous and fair as that wish is... There are certain things you have to feel, here. *(He presses his hand to his heart.)*

DOMENICO: *(Scrutinizing UMBERTO intently)* As for you, then, you don't feel this...er...desire, this need to call someone—me, for instance—father?

UMBERTO: I wouldn't want to lie to you, you deserve better than that of me, so—for now at least—I'll have to say— No!

DOMENICO: *(Is disappointed, and his interest shifts to RICCARDO)* What about you?

RICCARDO: The same with me.

DOMENICO: *(Turning his inquiring eyes on MICHELE)* And you?

MICHELE: *(Coming straight out with it)* Not me, Don Domenico.

DOMENICO: I see. *(He is discouraged.)* Such things come with time. You get used to them gradually. *(Cheering up a bit)* Well, boys, it's good to be with you, you're fine fellows, you all know how to look after yourselves. *(He is thinking hard now.)* One in one field, another in another, fine fellows! *(Turning abruptly on* UMBERTO*)* You work on a paper, don't you? From what they tell me, you're keen on your work, too, you take pride in it, you're a writer, you do articles...

UMBERTO: Short stories, too, once in a while.

DOMENICO: Stories, too. Your ambition is to be a great writer?

UMBERTO: Oh, I wouldn't say great.

DOMENICO: Why not? It's early days yet. *(Very interested now)* Of course, to succeed in a field like yours, you have to have it in you from the start, don't you? Genius has to run in the family, so to speak.

UMBERTO: I don't know if I do have it in me. You don't know how discouraged I get. I say to myself, "Umbe, don't fool yourself, this isn't what you're cut out for at all".

DOMENICO: *(Wonders now what he is cut out for)* Then what *is*? What do you really *like* to do?

UMBERTO: Lord knows! You have dreams of all sorts—when you're young.

RICCARDO: *(Rather grandly)* It's all coincidence. For instance: how is it I have a store in Via Chiaia? Because I made love to a girl. Because the girl was a shirtmaker. Because...

DOMENICO: *(Jumping at this chance)* You've made love to a lot of girls?

RICCARDO: So so. I've not done bad.

*(*DOMENICO*'s interest is aroused. He gets up to have a better look at* RICCARDO. *He is on the lookout for any gestures or inflection that he can attach to his own youth.)*

RICCARDO: Fact is, I have trouble finding the right type. I see a girl, I like her, I say, "That's for me, I'll marry her." But then I see another, and I seem to like her even more. I just can't explain it, there's always this other girl—the one I like better than the one I've got…

DOMENICO: *(Switching back to* UMBERTO*)* Whereas *you* keep calm. You don't lose your head about the girls. You think it over.

UMBERTO: Well, yes—and no. There isn't much to think over in the girls of today. There are good-looking girls everywhere. It's choosing that's hard. What can you do? You *have* to run through quite a few—just to find the one you really want!

*(*DOMENICO *concludes that there's the same tendency in* RICCARDO *as in* UMBERTO, *so he turns to* MICHELE.*)*

DOMENICO: *(To* MICHELE*)* What about you? Do you go for women?

MICHELE: I asked for trouble and I got it. I met my wife, and…good-bye, Michele! So now I live with both feet in one slipper. With my wife there's no fooling around, if you follow me: it isn't that I don't like the other girls, I don't like trouble, that's what…

DOMENICO: *(Discouraged)* So you like women, too. *(Pause. Now he's off on another tack.)* When I was a young fellow, I used to sing. We all used to get together, seven or eight of us. We used to go and serenade the ladies. Or we'd have supper on the terrace in summer, and the supper would turn into a concert, we'd sing Neapolitan songs to the mandolin or the guitar… Which of you can sing?

UMBERTO: I can't.

RICCARDO: Nor me neither.

DOMENICO: *(Happy at having eliminated two from the contest. To* MICHELE*)* And you?

MICHELE: I can! I couldn't work without it. I sing all the time!

DOMENICO: *(Getting excited)* Come on, then, let's hear you!

MICHELE: *(Already sorry he spoke up)* What shall I sing?

DOMENICO: Anything you like, go ahead, sing!

MICHELE: *(Swallowing hard)* I'm...er...ashamed!

DOMENICO: But you said you sang all the time!

MICHELE: I do. In the shop. Okay, you know "Monastery of Santa Chiara", it's good. *(He sings. His voice is negligible in volume and hideous in quality.)* "Munastero 'e Santa Chiara, tengo 'o core scuro scuro..."

RICCARDO: *(At a certain point interrupts him)* If that's singing, *I* can sing, too!

MICHELE: *(Insulted)* What d'you mean, *if* that's singing?

UMBERTO: So can I! If that's singing, *I* can sing!

DOMENICO: *(To RICCARDO)* Let's hear you first.

RICCARDO: Naw, naw, impossible, I don't have the gall he has, of course I know the tune...

(RICCARDO stops awkwardly. DOMENICO is silent, waiting for him to sing. So he strikes up.)

RICCARDO: "Munastero 'e Santa Chiara..."

(When he comes to the second line, UMBERTO joins in. MICHELE follows suit on the third. When they come to the top note of the song, loudly but not in unison and not together in rhythm, DOMENICO interrupts.)

DOMENICO: *(Roaring the first words after which they stop)* All right! *(Quietly)* That will do, thank you. *(Sighing)* Three Neapolitans, and not one of them can sing: what are we coming to?

(FILUMENA *comes in wearing lovely new clothes in comely colors. Skirt and blouse: the blouse of golden-yellow taffeta with flowers sewn into it, all this in two lighter tones, the skirt to be taffeta, too, but black. Her hair is piled high on her head in Neapolitan style. A few jewels, two ropes of pearls, a gold necklace, earrings. She looks almost youthful.*)

FILUMENA: You're just refusing to see it, Rosalia, it *is* wrong...

(TERESINA *comes in followed by* ROSALIA *and* LUCIA. *She is a dressmaker of the Neapolitan type. She is impassive, her customers' insults are just water on a duck's back, and her tranquility irritates.*)

TERESINA: It's all your imagination, Donna Filumena, and after all the years I've worked for you...

FILUMENA: You have the gall to say it's right when you know very well it's all wrong?

TERESINA: I should say it's all wrong just to please you, I suppose!

MICHELE: (*Approaching*) Hello—Mother!

UMBERTO: Hello—and congratulations.

RICCARDO: Congratulations!

FILUMENA: You're all here already? Hello! (*To* TERESINA*)* Now you know what's wrong with this skirt as well as I do: it's too tight! And why is it too tight? Because you didn't use enough silk. And why didn't you use enough silk? Because whenever you pick up a nice piece of silk, you cut a slice off for your little girl.

TERESINA: (*Bridling*) I do, do I?

FILUMENA: I was in your house myself, and I saw your little girl all dressed up in the silk you'd cut out of my skirt!

TERESINA: I'll really have to get mad at you, Donna Filumena! Course, if there's some left over, I'm not saying… But you're right, the customer comes first, that's always been my motto!

ROSALIA: Donna Filumena, you're the loveliest bride I ever saw!

FILUMENA: *(Shrilly)* I won't have you stealing from *me*, understand!

TERESINA: *(Imperturbable)* Now you're going *too* far, Donna Filumena! I swear by all that's holy…

DOMENICO: Filumena, can I speak to you for a moment?

FILUMENA: *(Limping a little in her new shoes)* Madonna, what shoes!

DOMENICO: Do they hurt? Maybe you should wear another pair.

FILUMENA: What is it you wanted to tell me?

DOMENICO: *(To* TERESINA*)* That'll be all for now, Teresina.

TERESINA: Yes, sir, I was just going. *(She folds the piece of cloth that she carries dresses in and puts it under her arm.)* And best wishes from your humble servant! *(Leaving upstage right, to* LUCIA*)* What was wrong with the dress, I'd like to know, why…

*(*TERESINA's *voice trails on until she is out of hearing.* LUCIA *has gone with her.)*

DOMENICO: *(To the three boys)* You boys go into the… er…drawing room and entertain the guests—let the revels commence! And you go with them, Rosalia.

ROSALIA: Yes, sir. *(To the boys)* Come along! *(Exits into the study)*

MICHELE: *(To the other two)* Come on!

RICCARDO: You've missed your vocation, you should have been a tenor at the San Carlo opera!

(They go into the study, laughing and talking.)

DOMENICO: *(After looking* FILUMENA *over)* You're
a beautiful woman, Filumena, and you're a *young*
woman, too, a slip of a girl. If I weren't such a confused
old slob…I know a man who could fall for you, hook,
line, and sinker.

FILUMENA: *(Already has guessed what is on* DOMENICO'*s
mind and doesn't want to discuss it)* Well, everything
seems to be in order now. I never thought it would be.

DOMENICO: *(Not to be deflected)* I'm not easy in my
mind, Filumena…

FILUMENA: How could either of us be easy in our
minds with only Lucia to depend on? Alfredo and
Rosalia are old…

DOMENICO: Don't change the subject, Filumena, you
know perfectly well what I'm getting at…. You can put
my mind at rest, you can bring me peace, Filumena.

FILUMENA: Can I?

DOMENICO: I've done everything you asked. After
the marriage was annulled, I came around to the
house—not once, many times, because you always
said you weren't home—I came and I said, "Filumena
Marturano, will you marry me?"

FILUMENA: And I said, "Domenico Soriano, I will".

DOMENICO: And now it's your wedding day, and
you're happy—I hope.

FILUMENA: I am happy.

DOMENICO: Then make *me* happy. Sit down, Filumena,
I have something to say. *(She sits.)* I wish you knew
how many times I've wanted to speak to you in these
last months. I couldn't, that's all, I was too shy or
embarrassed or something, I just couldn't. And for that
matter I couldn't bear to embarrass *you* and force you

to talk about things that…aren't easy to talk about. But
now we're to be man and wife. A boy and a girl think
they love each other when all they feel is an emotion
that can be exhausted by a single physical act, so they
get married. But the two people who're coming before
God this afternoon aren't children. They've *had* their
lives. I am fifty-two, you are forty-eight, we should
know what we're doing. *(Pause)* Now you do know
why you're marrying me. But I don't know why I'm
marrying you. I only know you said one of those boys
is my son.

FILUMENA: Is that your only reason for marrying?

DOMENICO: *(Gently)* No, it isn't. I'm terribly fond of
you, Filumena. We've been together twenty-five years.
Twenty-five years is a lifetime, a lifetime of memories,
yearnings…I found out for myself, I couldn't just cut
loose from it. Let me tell you my trouble, Filumena.
(Short pause) I don't sleep nights. Ten months have
passed since…that evening. And I've had no peace.
I don't sleep, I don't eat, I don't live. You know,
Filumena, I don't even breathe. I go like this… *(He
opens his mouth to take a deep breath of air.)* and the air
doesn't go down into my lungs, it stops here *(Pointing
to his throat)* You can't let this happen, Filumena,
you're a woman, you have a heart, you can't let this
happen. I remember your saying the day would come
when I'd want something from you and I mustn't
swear I'd refuse it, and I didn't swear, Filumena, and
the day *has* come, and I do want something from you,
as you hoped I would. I am on my knees before you,
Filumena, I kiss your hands, I kiss your clothes, and I
implore you: which is my son, my flesh, my blood?

(A very long pause)

FILUMENA: *(Still looking intently at her man)* I'll tell you:
it's that one. And now what happens? You'll pick "that

one" out, he'll be closer to you than the others, you'll
make sure he has a better future, and you'll figure out
how to make him richer...

DOMENICO: What if I do?

FILUMENA: *(With gentle cunning) Take* that one, then, he
certainly needs you, with his four kids...

DOMENICO: *(Very involved in this)* It's the...mechanic?

FILUMENA: *(Nodding)* The...hydraulic engineer, yes.

DOMENICO: *(Half to himself, getting progressively more
excited)* A good lad, well set up... But why did he get
married so young? With a little shop to take care of.... I
must take matters in hand. With a little capital he could
open a real repair shop, take on a few workers, learn to
boss the place, he needs some modern equipment... *(A
suspicion strikes him. Looking at* FILUMENA*)* Now look,
the plumber is the poorest of the lot, he's the one with
the family, he needs help...

FILUMENA: *(Pretending to be crestfallen)* What can a
mother do? She must help the weakest! But you didn't
believe me, you're too smart. What would you say to
Riccardo?

DOMENICO: The shirtmaker?

FILUMENA: *(Teasing him all the time)* No, no! It's
Umberto, the writer!

DOMENICO: *(Very put out and violent)* You're at it again!
Putting me against the wall! Crucifying me!

*(*FILUMENA, *touched by the tone of real trouble and
exhaustion in* DOMENICO's *voice, she tries to put her
innermost feelings into words, to find the formula, the
synthesis, which will make the situation clear to him:)*

FILUMENA: Listen to me, Domenico. And then let's
never speak of this again. *(The love she has held in so long
comes welling up.)* I always loved you with all my heart

and soul. In my eyes you were a god. And you are dear
to me still—perhaps dearer than ever. *(She breaks off,
thinking of his thoughtlessness, his failure to understand.)*
What have you done with your life? Did you want
to suffer? The Lord God gave you everything. Good
looks, good health, money…and me. I'd have done
anything for you. To save you the slightest pain I'd
have made a vow of perpetual silence and kept it! And
if you'd been…different, you'd have taken on three
children and thought nothing of it. But you were you.
(Pause) Never ask me again which is your son. I won't
tell. I can't tell. And you've got to be a gentleman and
not ask, or I might give way in a moment of weakness,
and that would be the end. Don't you see? I told you
it was the plumber, and within two seconds you were
talking about money, a little capital, a real repair
shop… You have money, you have a right to think of
it, but what would you think of next? "Why shouldn't
I tell him he's my son?" you'd think. "And who are
these two other chaps? Intruders!" An inferno. Brother
against brother. There'd be murder in this house,
Domenico. *(Pause)* Don't think of yourself, don't think
of me, Domenico. Think of them: it's the children
that count, Domenico. We must never forget it. When
they're tiny, we take them in our arms, we fret over
them when they're sick and can't explain what the
matter is. A little later, they come rushing at you with
their arms out, shouting: Papa! Then they come home
from school in winter with their hands freezing and
their noses running and asking if you've remembered
that surprise you promised… But when they're grown
up, when they're men, what are they? They're…just
sons. Or else enemies. I have three grown-up sons,
Domenico, decide whether you want them. You still
have time. And there'll be no ill feelings. We needn't
go through with this. If you say so, we're free to pick
up and go each his own way.

(The organ starts to play in the study.)

ROSALIA: *(Enters from the study followed by the three boys)* He's come! The holy priest is here!

(DOMENICO gets up and looks at them all very slowly. Provoked by FILUMENA's last remark, he is trying to force himself to break with her.)

DOMENICO: "We're free to pick up and go each his own way!" *(To the three boys)* I have something to say to you. *(Suspense)* I am a gentleman and I don't want to cheat you. Listen.

MICHEL, RICCARDO & UMBERTO: Yes, Father.

DOMENICO: *(For this "Yes, Father" has settled it)* Thank you, boys. I like the sound of that expression. I like it very much. *(Brightening up, now that this weight is off his mind)* Now, then, the usual thing is for the bride's father to take her to the altar. There are no parents with us today. There are sons, instead. Two of them will accompany the bride. The third, the bridegroom.

MICHELE: *(Firmly)* We'll go with mother. *(Inviting RICCARDO.)*

FILUMENA: *(Suddenly remembering)* What time is it?

RICCARDO: Five minutes to six.

(FILUMENA gives ROSALIA a meaningful look.)

ROSALIA: Don't worry. At six o'clock on the nose those candles will be lit!

FILUMENA: *(Leaning lovingly on MICHELE and RICCARDO)* Let's go in!

DOMENICO: *(To UMBERTO)* And you'll go with me.

(Forming a procession they go into the study. We hear the "Oh!" which greets the happy pair as they enter and the handclapping of the guests. ROSALIA stays in the dining room, watching the ceremony through the curtains, clapping

when the others clap, etc. We hear voices at first, then silence, then the wedding march. At this point ROSALIA *weeps copiously.* ALFREDO *comes in upstage right as if looking for somebody; he sees* ROSALIA *and goes over to her.* LUCIA *comes in and joins the other two.)*

(Here a change of lighting indicates a passage of time.)

*(*FILUMENA *comes in from the study, followed by* UMBERTO, MICHELE, *and* ROSALIA; *goes to sit downstage left.)*

FILUMENA: Phew, I'm tired!

MICHELE: You can rest now, Mamma. We'll be going. I have to work tomorrow.

ROSALIA: It was so lovely! May you live to be a hundred, child of mine, for child of mine you are and ever will be!

RICCARDO: *(Comes in from the study)* It *was* a lovely ceremony, too!

FILUMENA: *(Taking her shoes off and relaxing in her armchair)* Rosalia, bring me a glass of water, will you, dear?

ROSALIA: Oh, yes, Donna Filumena. *(Exit left)*

*(*DOMENICO *comes in from the study carrying a bottle of special white wine, the cork covered with sealing wax.)*

DOMENICO: No guests, no banquet, just a bottle of wine among the family. *(He takes a corkscrew and five glasses.)* The perfect nightcap. *(He uncorks the bottle.)*

ROSALIA: *(Comes in with a glass of water on a plate)* Here's the water.

DOMENICO: What do we want with *water*, for heaven's sake?

ROSALIA: It's for the signora!

DOMENICO: Tell the signora that water on an occasion of this sort is bad luck. Get two more glasses, and bring

Alfredo Amoroso, jockey and coachman, connoisseur of the racetrack.

ROSALIA: *(Calling)* Alfredo! Alfredo! Come and have some wine with your master! You, too, Lucia!

(ROSALIA brings DOMENICO two more glasses from a sideboard.)

ALFREDO: *(Coming in, followed by LUCIA)* Here I come!

DOMENICO: *(Has filled the glasses and now he is handing them around)* Here, Filumena, drink this. *(To the others)* Drink, everybody!

ALFREDO: Alla salute! *(He raises his glass.)*

DOMENICO: You remember the horses, don't you, Alfredo, the way they ran?

ALFREDO: *(Thrilled)* Madonna!

DOMENICO: They've stopped running. They stopped some time ago. I just didn't wish to believe it. And in my mind's eye I went on seeing them. But now I realize they stopped—a long time ago. *(Indicating the three boys)* It's their turn now. For them the race is just beginning. We'd better keep out of their way, you and I, Alfredo Amoroso, we can't compete with all this young blood.

ALFREDO: *(Quite overcome)* Madonna!

DOMENICO: Drink up, Alfredo.

(All drink.)

DOMENICO: I have just one thing left to say. It often happens in a family that a father with three or four children takes a special liking to one of them, maybe the ugly one, or the sick one, or the strong one, whichever it is, he's "father's boy", and the other kids don't mind. "Papa has a right to feel that way", they say. In our family this can never happen. Our family was…well, formed too late in the day. Maybe that's better. What I mean is, I'll still feel that special liking, but…I'll have to divide it among the three of you. So: *alia salute!*

(They drink.)

DOMENICO: Now, boys, tomorrow you're coming for dinner.

MICHELE, RICCARDO & UMBERTO: Thank you, Father.

RICCARDO: But now I'll be going. It's late, and Mamma needs a rest. Good-bye—and all the best!

UMBERTO: All the best!

MICHELE: And the same from me!

(They all kiss and embrace FILUMENA.*)*

UMBERTO: *(Coming over to Domenico, smiling affectionately)* Good night, Papa!

RICCARDO: G'night, Papa!

MICHELE: Sleep well, Papa!

DOMENICO: *(Is terribly happy. But one Italian custom remains)* Come on, boys! *(He stretches out his arms, embraces them, one after the other, kissing them on both cheeks)* Till tomorrow!

MICHELE, RICCARDO & UMBERTO: Till tomorrow!

(They leave upstage right, followed by ALFREDO, ROSALIA, *and* LUCIA.*)*

*(*DOMENICO *follows them out with his eyes, then thoughtfully returns to the table and pours himself some more wine.)*

FILUMENA: *(Is still sitting in the armchair, has changed her shoes)* Madonna, how tired I am! It comes over me all at once.

DOMENICO: *(Understanding, lovingly)* You've been on your feet all day. And with all the strain of it! Now you can rest. *(He takes his glass over to the terrace.)* What a lovely evening!

(FILUMENA has been feeling something in her throat that makes her groan slightly: at any rate a sound like sobbing comes out of her. Her eyes are staring out into nothingness. She seems to expect something. Her face is lined with tears.)

DOMENICO: *(Concerned, comes over)* What's the matter, dear?

FILUMENA: *(With deep joy)* I'm crying, Domenico, I'm crying! And, oh, how sweet it is to cry!

DOMENICO: *(Holding her lovingly to him)* You'll be all right, Filumena, you'll be all right. You've done some running in your time, too, it's been a hard race, there's been a fall or two, but you always picked yourself up again somehow. And now it's time for a rest. *(He returns to the table for yet another glass of wine.)* A mother's a mother, and sons are sons, Filumena Soriano.

(DOMENICO is drinking as the curtain falls.)

END OF PLAY

www.ingramcontent.com/pod-product-compliance
Lightning Source LLC
Chambersburg PA
CBHW052211090426
42741CB00010B/2494